T0147785

Character
Makes the Man

Character
Makes the Man

Kentucky Military Institute, 1845-1971

Tommy R. Young II

Order this book online at www.trafford.com
or email orders@trafford.com

Most Trafford titles are also available at major online book retailers.

© Copyright 2013 Tommy R. Young II.
All rights reserved. No part of this publication may be reproduced, stored in a retrieval
system, or transmitted, in any form or by any means, electronic, mechanical, photocopying,
recording, or otherwise, without the written prior permission of the author.

Printed in the United States of America.

ISBN: 978-1-4907-1205-5 (sc)
ISBN: 978-1-4907-1207-9 (hc)
ISBN: 978-1-4907-1206-2 (e)

Library of Congress Control Number: 2013914836

Trafford rev. 09/06/2013

 www.trafford.com

North America & international
toll-free: 1 888 232 4444 (USA & Canada)
fax: 812 355 4082

CONTENTS

This work is dedicated to the more than 11,000 cadets who attended

Kentucky Military Institute

ACKNOWLEDGMENTS

———⋅•⋅———

N o project such as this history is possible without the assistance and support of a number of individuals.

Special thanks go to a number of KMI cadets who contributed newspapers, catalogs, yearbooks, photographs, encouragement, and stories: Park A. Shaw, 1942; Larry Arrowood, 1956; Jack Morgan, 1957; Elden Durand, 1959; Jim McDonald, 1948; Leon Hirsh, 1968; Charles Claibourne, 1959; Chris Crawford, 1961; Al Bender, 1960; Gerry Brinker, 1959; John Beard, 1959; Jim Flora, 1962; Kennedy Simpson, 1971; Ben Kaufmann, 1961; Jim Tullis, 1959; Herschel Murray, 1955; Richard Stephenson, 1958; Norvin Green, 1950; Bernard Dahlem, 1946; and Dick Hammack, 1948. To the former cadet who said, "Write the damn thing while some of us are still alive," here it is.

Ann Beard Thompson and John A. Beard, who contributed a number of items from their father, Allen Murray Beard, 1922, and uncle, Benjamin Franklin Beard, 1916.

Ellen Brinker, who contributed items from her husband, Gerry Brinker, 1959.

Five former members of the faculty provided information and insights about their time at KMI: Donald A. Seibert, Charles "Alex" Hodgin, William T. Simpson, Frank Kern, and Ben Hewes.

Ann Flotte, who supplied photographs and information concerning KMI's time in Eau Gallie.

Alec and Sarah Poff, who sent materials found in Lieutenant Colonel Ernest Poff's files.

Brad Lyman, James Elliott, and Chris Brice and the library staff at Kentucky Country Day who made the resources of the school available to the author.

Sandra Bell and the staff of the Stewart Home School, who allowed the author open access to the school's facilities.

Glenda Stephens, for an extensive card file and Jim's notes.

Dorothy Korwek and the staff of the City of Venice Archives and Area Historical Collection, now known as the Venice Museum and Archives under the direction of James Hagler, who found countless items in the collection and scanned a large number of photographs.

Cindy Shyrock and the family of Miss Mary Reichspfarr, who sent the author a number of items from Miss Mary's estate.

Betty Kay Hammock Utley, who contributed a number of movies taken by her father and supplied the interesting perspective of a young woman growing up on the KMI campus with countless "brothers."

Three faculty members deserve special mention: Bartley Williams, Ben Hewes, and Donald Seibert. Black Bart apparently saw something in a rambunctious, headstrong, hard-to-manage cadet that others missed and frequently gave him the benefit of the doubt. Ben Hewes pointed a young boy down a career path that he has followed for more than fifty years. Until his death, he continued to counsel and encourage the author in his work. Don Seibert enthusiastically supported the author's efforts. He would strongly object to the characterization, but he might well have been the embodiment of "Character Makes the Man."

Finally, Joyce, my wife of more than forty-seven years, deserves special thanks. Through all the years, she has been the rock that brought stability and purpose to the author's life. She has attended reunions, sorted through archival materials, and listened to countless stories without complaining. Without her support and encouragement, this history would never have seen the light of day. Everyone who has found any value or enjoyment in this history owes her a hearty thank you, as do I.

INTRODUCTION

Try to remember the kind of September when life was slow and
oh, so mellow
Try to remember the kind of September when grass was green and
grain was yellow
Try to remember the kind of September when you were a tender
and callow fellow
Try to remember, and if you remember
Then follow

—"Try to Remember," from the *Fantasticks*,
lyrics by Tom Jones

Follow me through the history of an institution that was more than just a school, an institution that left an indelible mark on more than 11,000 young men and their families, an institution that educated and trained young men to be valuable members of society for 126 years.

My wife, Joyce, and I returned to Lyndon in May of 1973 for the final commencement of Kentucky Academy. I had not been back to Lyndon since I graduated in 1959. We were living in Louisiana, but something told me that I had to go to Lyndon. We made a special trip home for the final commencement. There were no cadet MPs giving us directions, so after finding a parking place, we walked toward the gym. It was strange not to see cadets in dress uniforms, just students in blazers. At the door to the gym stood a familiar figure, Sergeant Alfred O. Drury, who had been a member of the Military Department when I was a cadet. His comment after fourteen years was "Young, what the hell are you doing back on campus?" I ignored his remark and said simply, "Good morning, Sergeant."

We were standing at the back of the gym trying to decide where to sit when I felt someone touch my hand. I looked down to see Bart Williams, Black Bart, the nemesis of my cadet years. He looked at me, gently squeezed my arm, and said softly, "Welcome home, Mr. Young."

I am now retired and live in the house that I left more than fifty-eight years ago to become a KMI cadet. It took a number of years to realize that Bart was right. I had come home.

That home is now gone. It exists only as a memory for a diminishing number of men. However, what that institution tried to achieve, through the efforts of a highly dedicated staff and faculty, should not be lost to history. The young boys who grew to manhood on the various KMI campuses learned important lessons about life and the world. But more importantly, they learned about themselves. They learned that "Character Makes the Man" is more than just a motto.

Chapter I

---◆---

THE EARLY YEARS

Located in the rolling hills about six miles from Frankfort, the property purchased by Colonel Allen in 1845 had originally been developed by Edmond Scanland and was known as Farmdale. It is believed that Scanland was the first to discover the reported medical powers of a mineral spring located on the property. He boiled the water and produced mineral salts which he sold locally. In 1838, Dr. Joseph G. Roberts purchased the property from Scanland and constructed a number of buildings to accommodate guests. The following year, he announced the opening of a spa known as Franklin Springs. When initially opened, the spa could accommodate about one hundred guests. By 1840, the facilities had been expanded to accommodate between two hundred and three hundred guests. Unfortunately for Dr. Roberts and his business venture, a rumor began to circulate that the springs had become contaminated, and people ceased to patronize the spa in significant numbers. For a short time, the facilities were used as a school for young ladies. However, that venture failed, and the property reverted to Mr. Scanland. In the summer of 1842, the property was used for a Presbyterian camp meeting.

Apparently, the spa still attracted some guests. In 1843, Robert T. P. Allen, a professor at Transylvania College in Lexington, and his wife, Julia Ann, spent some time at the spa. Allen resigned his position in 1845 and purchased the Franklin Springs property and opened a school known as the Franklin Institute. At some point, the buildings that had been erected by the Springs Company were destroyed by a fire. Allen would replace them with new buildings; the main building would resemble the State Capital building in Frankfort.[1]

Franklin Institute opened in 1846 and was the first military school in what was considered the West. Only three other military schools were in existence when Allen began his venture. The United States Military Academy at West Point, New York, had been established in 1802; Norwich University, Northfield, Vermont, had been founded in 1819 and chartered in 1834; and Virginia Military Institute at Lexington, Virginia, had been founded by the State of Virginia in 1839.[2]

By the time he purchased the property at Farmdale, Allen had already had a varied career. He was born in Maryland on September 26, 1813, and entered the United States Military Academy in 1830. He graduated fifth in his class in 1834 and then served as a lieutenant in the Topographical Corps during the Second Seminole War before resigning his commission. He received an appointment as a civil agent to oversee harbor improvements on Lake Erie. After only two years, he left that position to become an ordained Methodist Episcopal minister. He moved to Meadville, Pennsylvania, where he occupied the chair of mathematics and civil engineering at Allegany College from 1838 to 1841. In 1841, he accepted the same position at Transylvania College in Lexington, Kentucky.

During his freshman year at West Point, Allen was expelled for "conduct unbecoming a cadet and insubordination." His expulsion was the result of his refusal to name the other cadets involved in the burning of an unsightly building on the academy grounds. Feeling that he had been treated unfairly, Allen went to Washington to personally plead his case before President Andrew Jackson. Jackson was so impressed by the young man, Allen would have been about eighteen years old, that he ordered him reinstated at the academy.

James Stephens relates that Allen met his future wife, Julia A. Dickinson, the president's niece, in Washington. In a statement by Carol Allen Gibson, the great-great-granddaughter of Allen, she argues that Ms.

---

[1] William T. Simpson, "A History of the Kentucky Military Institute during the Nineteenth Century, 1845-1900," p. 14. Hereinafter cited as Simpson.

[2] National Register of Historic Places Inventory, Nomination Form, Stewart Home School, June 3, 1976. The Nomination Form gives the name of the founder as Edmond Scanland while other sources list his name as Scanlan.

Dickinson was not the niece of President Jackson. The president's niece was actually Julia Bond. Ms. Dickinson's mother was married to Jacob Dickinson, and she was a Bond. There is also some confusion about what the *P* stood for in Allen's name. Various sources give it as Pitcairn, Pritchard, and Pritchett. The most accepted of the names is Pitcairn.[3]

Colonel Allen picked an opportune time to begin his military school. In the decade prior to his decision, there was a belief throughout the country that West Point was an "aristocratical institution," and it should be abolished. In 1836, Kentucky congressman Albert G. Hawes had suggested that West Point should be abolished. That same year, there was a failed effort to create a professor of civil and military engineering at Transylvania. However, attitudes concerning military education began to shift in Kentucky. However, opinions changed; and in 1842, Transylvania began a course of military training. The people of Kentucky appeared to be anxious to make military training available to the young men of the state. In just five more years, the legislature would charter KMI. It appears that military education was acceptable if it was available to a large number of students and was not "aristocratical."[4]

Colonel R. T. P. Allen,
Founder of Kentucky
Military Institute—Venice

Allen's resignation from his position at Transylvania brought a letter from Henry Clay in which he lamented the loss of Allen as a faculty member. However, Clay wished Allen the best of luck in his venture at Franklin Springs. He

3   James D. Stephens, *Reflections: A Portrait-Biography of the Kentucky Military Institute (1845-1971)*, p. 1. Hereinafter cited as Stephens. http://www.usgennet.org/usa/ky/county/franklin/indea/KMI.html; http://www.angelfire.com/tx/randystexas/page78.html; An obituary of Mrs. Allen reported that she was the niece of President Jackson and they were married in the White House. http://www.joycetice.com/clippings/tcobt386.htm.

4   Rod Andrew, Jr., *Long Gray Lines: The Southern Military School Tradition, 1839-1915*, Chapel Hill: University of North Carolina Press, 2001, pp. 15-16.

also informed Allen that he could use his name as a reference in advertising the new school.[5]

The purpose of the new school, as stated by Colonel Allen in 1845, was "The principal will aim, not to render to his pupils a mere magazine of knowledge, but so to implant useful information as to develop and give direction to the mental faculties and physical powers, that the pupil, having acquired correct habits of thought and observation, may afterwards pursue his search for knowledge independently, and be able to turn it to practical account." Under his system, Colonel Allen intended to educate "the entire man, MORAL, INTELLECTUAL AND PHYSICAL."[6] The colonel hoped to found a school based upon the full curriculum of the best colleges in the United States, with the addition of the discipline practiced at West Point.

In an undated letter to "The Friends and Patrons of the Kentucky Military Institute," Colonel Allen stated his view of the importance of military discipline in the education of young men:

> The Superintendent would respectfully submit that he has been long convinced from the experience of many years' teaching in Colleges, of the absolute necessity of a stronger and more rigid government, and a closer watch care than can be exercised in the ordinary College; hence the establishment of the Kentucky Military Institute, whose government is reinforced by the strong arm of Military Law. The history of the Institute, thus far, in a success wholly unprecedented, has demonstrated the accuracy of this conviction. The authorities of the Institute are determined that nothing shall be left undone, on their part, to render the Institute all that its warmest friends can desire.

Colonel Allen then solicited information concerning whether the friends and patrons would be sending their sons to KMI for the next term. The accommodations for the cadets had barely been adequate to house the students the previous term. Some of the existing rooms were not "fit for occupancy" in the coming term. The colonel was planning

---

[5] Simpson, op. cit., p. 15.

[6] National Register of Historic Places Inventory, Nomination Form, Stewart Home School, June 3, 1976.

to erect additional and permanent barracks, and he wanted to be sure he constructed enough rooms to house both new and returning cadets. He also asked that the recipients of the letter urge parents of prospective students to submit their applications as quickly as possible.[7]

The campus of the new school was described by one observer:

> The location of the institute is a beautiful one, and is reached by an hour's ride by stage from the State Capital over the Frankfort and Harrodsburg Turnpike. The buildings were erected at a cost of $100,000 and are admirably adapted to school purposes. They are heated by steam and lighted by gas, and the excellent taste displayed in arrangement of buildings and grounds commends the establishment to visitors as a place of unequaled beauty.[8]

On Monday, April 6, 1846, thirty young men arrived to begin classes at the Franklin Institute. The faculty consisted of three men: Colonel Allen, who would teach mathematics and natural science; Francis A. Hall, taught ancient languages and literature; and Martin S. Harmon, who taught French and German as well as English literature. Patrons were assured by Allen that additional faculty members would be added as needed. The student's day began at five o'clock in the morning and was filled with activity until taps sounded at ten in the evening. Such schedules were common in all military schools and were intended to curtail behavior problems as well as instill discipline in the daily lives of the cadets. In 1856, the KMI Board of Visitors stated that "no cadet can, with impunity, absent himself for a single hour without the consent of some member of the Faculty." [9]

Originally, the main building could only house fifty students, but it was expanded with the addition of 24 rooms in 1847. The following year, additional buildings were constructed to accommodate the growing number of students. A building with an additional 40 rooms was

---

7   Undated letter from Colonel R. T. P. Allen to Friends and Patrons of Kentucky Military Institute.

8   Simpson, op. cit., p. 12.

9   Quoted in Jennifer R. Green, *Military Education and the Emerging Middle Class in the Old South*, New York, Cambridge University Press, 2008, p. 63.

constructed as well as a chapel and a dining room. The addition of these rooms brought the number of students that could be accepted to 160. When completed, the buildings enclosed almost an acre of ground, and all rooms opened upon a central court.[10]

Colonel Allen's founding of KMI was all part of a trend in the southern states. The historian Bruce Alardice states that between 1827 and 1860, there were ninety-six military colleges, academies, and universities that operated on the military system founded in the slave states. At the same time, there were only fifteen such schools founded in the Free states.[11] The system of education advocated by Colonel Allen was gaining acceptance throughout the country. "Advocates of the military system of education continued to stress its other merits (imparting discipline, character, and health), and many civilian educators were beginning to listen."[12]

Barracks and Courtyard Today—Young

Initially, Allen hoped to place his school on the same relationship with the State of Kentucky as that enjoyed by Virginia Military Institute. However, after discussions with various prominent Kentuckians, he decided that state financial support was highly unlikely. He then proposed a plan to the state legislature that would allow the use of the school's facilities by the state while the school would be named Kentucky Military Institute. Under the terms of Allen's proposal, the school would remain a private institution while the state would furnish its military equipment and supervise its military organization.

---

[10] National Register of Historic Places Inventory, Nomination Form, Stewart Home School, June 3, 1976. Simpson, p. 26.

[11] Bruce Allardice, "West Points of the Confederacy: Southern Military Schools and the Confederate Army." *Civil War History* 43, no. 4, December 1997, p. 330.

[12] Rod Andrews, *Long Gray Lines: The Southern Military School Tradition, 1839-1915*, Chapel Hill, University of North Carolina Press, 2001, pp. 20-21.

On January 20, 1847, an act was approved which incorporated Kentucky Military Institute. The act essentially followed Allen's proposal: the state would furnish the school's military equipment, and the governor would appoint a nine-member board of visitors, to be headed by the state adjutant general. The board of visitors would conduct an annual inspection of the school to ensure the proper maintenance of the public arms at the school and that the operation of the school and the performance of the faculty were satisfactory. The board was to report annually to the governor on its findings. The legislation provided that any commissioned officer in the state militia could attend the institute for a period not to exceed ten months without charge. Kentucky Military Institute would remain a strictly private business, and the state would have only an advisory function.[13]

Colonel Allen informed the board of visitors in his report of June 16, 1847, that:

> The Institute, by the act of incorporation is, "de facto" a State institution: the fact that the property is in private hands in no wise detracting from its public character, more than if the same property were held by the Board of Visitors under lease.
>
> The Regulations adopted by your Board for the government of the Institute have been published and extensively circulated, and it is deemed unnecessary to refer to them here, further than to say that they are essentially identical with those governing the United States Military Academy at west Point, enjoining, however, a course of study more extensive in natural science and belles-letters than that taught at that honored institution.[14]

The report stated that there were forty-nine cadets present at the end of the year. All but one cadet, who was from Tennessee, were from the state of Kentucky. By the end of the next year, there were 100 cadets in attendance, representing seven states: Kentucky, Tennessee, Texas, Louisiana, Mississippi, Iowa, and the Indian Territory. In 1848, there were 120 cadets enrolled, and the states of Maryland and Georgia joined

---

[13] Simpson, op. cit., pp. 18-19; Stephens, op. cit., p. 2.
[14] Quoted in 1908 *Saber*, p. 9.

the list of states represented by the cadet corps. It was noted that the commandant was having difficulty in erecting new barracks fast enough to accommodate the rapidly increasing enrollment.[15]

The curriculum of KMI under Colonel R. T. P. Allen resembled the educational system advocated by Alden Partridge. A graduate of West Point in 1806 and its superintendent for a decade beginning in 1808, Partridge became an advocate of what he called an American system of education. After resigning his commission in 1818, Partridge established the American Literary, Scientific and Military Academy, the present-day Norwich University, at Norwich, Connecticut. Partridge hoped to educate students "to discharge in the best possible manner, the duties they owe to themselves, to their fellow-man, and to their country." During his lifetime, Partridge established six other military academies in addition to the one at Norwich, and his students established even more schools across the nation.[16]

There is no evidence that Colonel Allen had any contact with Partridge, but there are many threads of his system in the KMI curriculum. Although Partridge died in 1854, there were even more elements of the Partridge system in the KMI curriculum implemented by Colonel C. W. Fowler in the early twentieth century. Partridge believed that the military education his academies offered was only supplemental to the civilian part of the curriculum. He argued that the existing educational system ignored the important elements of agriculture, commerce, and manufacturing. He expanded the traditional college curriculum "by making it more practical, scientific, and truly liberal. He expanded the classical curriculum to include modern languages and history as well as political economy and engineering. Indeed, Partridge's institution was the first in the United States to offer instruction in civil engineering." Partridge was also a lifelong advocate of the benefits of physical education for his students. Strenuous outdoors work, including long marches by the students, was typical of the activities he advocated.[17]

---

[15] Ibid.

[16] Gary Thomas Lord, History of Norwich University: Images of Its Past, http://www.norwich.edu/about/history.html, . . http://en.wikipedia.org/wiki/Alden_Partridge.

[17] Ibid. For a detailed discussion of Partridge's ideas on education see *The American Journal of Education*, Vol. 23, edited by Henry Bernard, pp. 833-864.

In 1849, Colonel Allen resigned as superintendent of KMI and accepted a federal appointment as special agent with the Post Office Department. Whether it was Allen's restless nature or the fact that he had greatly overextended himself and was deep in debt or some combination of the two factors that caused him to resign will never be known. Rather than lose everything, he devised a plan where the school would be turned over to a board composed of his creditors. In his new position with the Post Office, he was responsible for all mail services in California and Oregon. Allen lost his position after the death of President Zachary Taylor, when President Millard Fillmore removed many of Taylor's appointees and replaced them with his own supporters. Allen remained in California as the successful owner and publisher of the *Pacific News*, a newspaper he started at some point during his stay in California.

When Allen resigned as superintendent, the board of visitors selected Francis W. Capers to head the school. The new superintendent would answer to the school's creditors. At the time of his selection, Capers was teaching ancient languages and literature at Transylvania. Before coming to Transylvania, Capers had been an original member of the faculty at the Citadel in Charleston, South Carolina, as a professor of mathematics. In 1848, Capers had resigned his position at the Citadel and moved to Frankfort. As soon as he was appointed superintendent, he changed the name of the school to Kentucky Collegiate and Military Institute and began working to put the school on the same footing as VMI and the Citadel. These schools and many other military schools established in the South received various amounts of state funding for cadets in order for them to receive an education. Many "state military schools in the antebellum South put systems in place that financed at least one student per senatorial district."[18]

Writing about state-supported military schools, historian Rod Andrew drew a conclusion that could also be applied to KMI. "Expand the scope of higher education into the sciences, democratize higher education through a unique student aid program for poorer scholars, increase the number of qualified school teachers, and produce a more enlightened and public minded citizenry." Although there is no evidence that KMI ever received

---

[18]   Green, op. cit., p. 39.

any state funds for students' tuition, the other benefits cited by Andrews were definitely a part of the legacy of KMI.[19]

Students who received financial assistance from the state were known as state cadets, as opposed to pay cadets. The "state cadets" were normally required to perform certain duties while cadets and frequently had an obligation to teach in the state for a specific number of years after graduation. The Louisiana State Legislature approved the payment of boarding expenses for 150 cadets known as beneficiary cadets. "This arrangement offered the best public funding for southern higher schools at a time when no southern state maintained a functioning public school system."[20]

Before Capers could put KMI on the same footing as VMI and the Citadel, Colonel Allen returned from California and managed to regain his position as owner and superintendent. He immediately changed the name of the school back to Kentucky Military Institute. There is no evidence as to how Allen was able to make enough money in California in a little more than a year to pay his creditors.[21]

Colonel Capers returned to Charleston, South Carolina, where he became superintendent of the Citadel, a position he held for six years. Capers resigned his position at the Citadel and accepted the same position at Georgia Military Institute in Marietta, Georgia. Cadets from GMI were drill instructors for various Confederate Army units and participated in one battle during the Civil War. The empty campus was burned by General Sherman's troops on November 15, 1864. Following the war, the school was not rebuilt. General Capers died in 1896 in Charleston, South Carolina.[22]

---

[19] Andrews, op. cit., p. 24.

[20] Green, Jennifer R., *Military Education and the Emerging Middle Class in the Old South*, New York, Cambridge University Press, 2008, pp. 39-40, and http://www.lsu.edu/visitors/history.shtml.

[21] Stephens speculates that Allen received financial assistance from his brother-in-law, Jay Cooke. However, there is no direct evidence to support that speculation, op. cit., p. 2.

[22] Stephens, op. cit., p. 14, mistakenly says that Capers was not employed by the Citadel in 1851,. http://en.wikipedia.org/wiki/Georgia_Military_Institute, http://www.citadel.edu/root/presidents, http://www.citadel.edu/root/brief-history.

Colonel Capers's management of the school had been excellent, and the school continued to grow. In 1850, there were 150 students enrolled. In 1851, the first graduating class of 4 members from the college division received their AB degrees. All 4 would remain at KMI and receive the AM degree within the next 2 years. The more successful of these first graduates was John G. Carlisle, who would serve in the Kentucky Legislature as the lieutenant governor, speaker of the House of Representatives, U.S. senator, and secretary of the Treasury.[23] Robert J. Adcock, another of the 1851 graduates, would teach mathematics, astronomy, and mechanical arts at KMI until the outbreak of the Civil War.[24] After Allen's return, the school continued to prosper, and seven cadets graduated in 1852. That same year, tuition was raised to $165 a year. The number of graduates in 1853 was fourteen. In 1854, the number of students dropped to 139, and the number of graduates fell to 12.[25]

Although Colonel Allen was back in control of the school, he felt the need to bring in another person to help manage the school. He selected Edwin W. Morgan to join him as joint superintendent. Morgan was born on April 11, 1811, and was appointed to the United States Military Academy in 1833. He graduated in 1837 and was promoted to the rank of second lieutenant in the artillery. He served in the Second Seminole War from 1837 to 1838. He was promoted to first lieutenant in July 1838. Morgan resigned from the army in 1839 and became the principal assistant engineer

The campus in 1854—Bender

---

23   William Simpson says that none of the four were from Kentucky and cites the Catalogue of the Kentucky Military Institute for 1857, op. cit., p. 31. He gives the names in academic order as R.J. Adcock, Ohio; A.G. Gower, Iowa; William P.S. Duncan; and John G. Carlisle, Ohio. However, Carlisle's biographies state that he was born in Kentucky, http://bioguide.congress.gov/scripts/biodisplay.pl?index+C000152. James Stephens lists Carlisle as an 1858 graduate, Stephens, op. cit., p. 42.

24   Stephens, op. cit., p. 46.

25   Simpson, op. cit., pp. 32-33.

of the State of Pennsylvania for the next seven years. He rejoined the army as a major in 1847 and served during the Mexican War until he left the army as a lieutenant colonel in 1848.

Morgan was superintendent of Western Military Institute, Blue Licks, Kentucky, from 1849 to 1851. He then assumed the position of chief engineer of Shelby Railroad, Kentucky, from 1852 to 1854. During that same period, he was vice president of Shelby College, Kentucky. In 1854, Colonel Allen brought Colonel Morgan in as joint superintendent of KMI.[26]

Main Building and Cadets—Young

The report of the board of visitors in 1854 was filled with glowing praise for Colonel Allen and KMI. The board pointed out that:

> The "military feature" of the Institute should be understood and appreciated.
>
> It is not so much to impart military knowledge as to receive the advantage of discipline and habits of subordination, that tactics are taught. The military drill occupies but one hour in the day, after the daily collegiate studies have been concluded, and is practiced because it is conducive to manly exercise, good health, and gentlemanly carriage. It is never permitted to interfere with the regular studies of the cadet.[27]

The board found that the course of study was very extensive and was equal to, if not more thorough, than any college with which they were

---

[26] Cullum, Biographical Register of Officers and Graduates of the U. S. Military Academy at West Point, hereafter cited as Cullum; Mable Alstetter and Gladys Watson, "Western Military Institute, 1847-1861," *Filson Club Historical Quarterly*, 10, April, 1936, pp. 100-115.

[27] Catalogue of the Officers and Cadets of the Kentucky Military Institute, from September 12, 1853 to June 14, 1854, Frankfort, A. G. Hughes & Co., 1854, p. 12.

familiar. They specifically noted that civil engineering was especially well taught and qualified the cadets for profitable employment immediately upon graduation.

Synopsis of Course of Study—1854
Preparatory Course

Arithmetic, Book-keeping, Algebra commenced, Latin Grammar,
Latin Lessons, Caesar's Commentaries, Ovid and Sallust.
Regular Course

Freshman

First Session
1. Algebra
2. Virgil: Cicero's Orations
3. English Grammar reviewed
4. English Synonyms
5. Duties of Soldier

Second Session
1. Algebra reviewed
2. Geometry
3. Cicero's Oration's continued
4. Parker's Aids to Composition
5. Duties of Soldier

Sophomore

1. Trigonometry, Plane and Spherical Mensuration and Surveying with Field Practice and Topography; Descriptive Geometry
2. Horace; Latin Composition; Greek and French Elective
3. Anatomy and Physiology
4. Botany
5. Duties of Soldier

1. Analytical Geometry; Shades and Shadows, Perspective and Linear Drawing
2. De Senectute, De Amicitia, etc.; Tacotus—Greek and French Elective
3. Rhetoric and Elocution
4. Comparative Anatomy and Natural Theology
5. Duties of Soldier

Junior

1. Calculus, Differential and Integral

1. Principles of Mechanics and Construction

⋄ 13 ⋄

2. Cicero de Oratore; Elements of Criticism; Greek and French Elective
3. Chemistry
4. Electricity, Magnetism, and Electro-Magnetism
5. Duties of non-commissioned officers—use of sword

2. Juvenal Intellectual and Moral Philosophy, Greek and French Elective
3. Zoology; Mineralogy
4. Optics, Pneumatics, Drawing
5. Duties of non-commissioned officers—use of sword

Senior

1. Astronomy, Geodetic Surveying and Navigation, with spherical projections and mapping
2. Architecture and Engineering, with Drawing
3. Geology and Mines
4. Bayard on the Constitution
5. Duties of Commissioned Officers—use of sword

1. Engineering, with field practice and drawing
2. Political Economy
3. Outlines of History
4. Vattel's Law of Nations
5. Duties of Commissioned Officers—use of sword

The school year that ended in June of 1854 was the best year in the school's brief history. At the beginning of the year, 139 students were enrolled. By the end of the year, there were 117 students, representing fourteen states and two foreign countries. Colonel Allen intended to introduce a more thorough study of physiology, zoology, mineralogy, and French in the near future. The cadets were housed, two men to a room, in new brick barracks that were heated by steam. Overall, the cadets had been healthy during the year with no deaths or serious illnesses. The cadets were required to attend prayer services every morning and public worship on Sunday. The services were conducted in the school's chapel and sectarianism was carefully avoided.[28]

The financial activities of the cadets were closely regulated by the school. Funds were deposited with the school treasurer:

---

[28] Ibid., p. 14.

The Treasurer will keep an account with each Cadet, in which he will be credited with the sums deposited, and charged with the sums paid to his creditors; and for such disbursements proper receipts shall be taken by the Treasurer and kept on file in his office. He shall make annually to the Board a full report of the amount of expenditure of each Cadet, and every liability to and by the Institute.

No Cadet shall contract any debt without permission of the Superintendent; nor be furnished with any article whatever, by any storekeeper or other person, without his order.

Every Cadet shall keep a book, in which shall be charged every article he may purchase; and such purchase must have the Superintendent's authorization written therein.

No Cadet shall obtain from the Superintendent an order for goods or money, unless there be a balance due to the said Cadet, in the hands of the Treasurer, equal to the amount of such order.[29]

Following the 1854 commencement, Colonel Allen decided to retire and become a farmer. He sold his holdings to Colonel Morgan and moved to the home he had constructed just outside Frankfort. Colonel Morgan purchased all of the buildings and 256 acres from Allen. As with most of his ventures, Allen's stint as a farmer only lasted three years before he moved to Bastrop, Texas. Allen, always the educator, established Bastrop Military Institute, which opened about 1858. The school saw continual growth until the outbreak of the Civil War, when enrollment dropped drastically. Colonel Allen was placed in charge of Camp Clark, a training camp for Texas recruits. He would command the Fourth Texas Infantry Regiment, a part of Hood's Texas Brigade, but Allen was not acceptable to the men of the regiment. Many of the men had been at Camp Clark and considered Allen to be a martinet, and they literally drove him out of camp. Allen would return to Bastrop, where he recruited the Seventeenth Texas Infantry Regiment, which he commanded until November 1863.

---

[29] Ibid., 16.

At that time, he was placed in command of Camp Ford, a prisoner of war camp near Tyler, Texas.[30]

One of the most persistent problems that plagued KMI over the years was fire. In December of 1855, a fire destroyed most of the administration building, the dining room, and the kitchen. About $17,000 in insurance money was collected and a rebuilding program was started

Old Barracks—Kaufmann

immediately. Although the rebuilding was completed the next year, a number of applications had to be rejected because of a lack of room for additional students. The rebuilding process gave Colonel Morgan the opportunity to exercise his interest in architecture. He was an advocate of what he called useful education, which included architecture, construction, and design. He had published two highly detailed lithographs which were titled *Parallel of the Orders of Architecture.* According to the nomination form for the National Historic Register, features of the rebuilt main building include "a pair of bay windows, the cupola, and interior decorations that have a definite mid-Victorian Italianate flavor."[31]

One rule that would not change from the time KMI opened until it closed was that the use of alcoholic beverages by cadets was always prohibited. The school imposed stiff penalties on any cadet found drinking or in possession of alcohol up to and including expulsion. In an effort to make it

KMI Library Today at
Frankfort—Young

---

[30]   http://www.texansinthecivilwar.com/colonel_allen.html; http://www.tshaon line.org/handbook/online/articles.

[31]   Simpson, op. cit., p. 41; National Register of Historic Places Inventory, Nomination Form, Stewart Home School, June 3, 1976.

more difficult for cadets to obtain alcohol, the Kentucky Legislature passed a law in 1858 that "made it an offense and provided for a fine of ten dollars for the selling or giving liquor to a Kentucky Military Institute cadet." The law also stipulated that merchants could not recover the cost of goods sold to cadets under the age of twenty.[32]

Kentucky Military Institute's reputation as an outstanding military school was wide spread by 1859. William T. Sherman, newly appointed superintendent of the Seminary of Learning of the State of Louisiana, the future Louisiana State University, a school with a military system of government, paid a visit to Frankfort.[33] He

Main Building as it Exists Today at Frankfort—Young

was collecting information on the operation of three military schools, the United States Military Academy, Virginia Military Institute, and KMI. In addition, Sherman planned to visit George B. McClellan, president of the Illinois Central Railroad in Chicago to find out what he had learned about the military schools in Europe when he was an observer during the Crimean War. Sherman was familiar with the situation at West Point, and he had requested information from the superintendent of VMI, Francis H. Smith. Sherman and Colonel Morgan conferred on a

Four Cadets from 1847-1854—Kaufmann

---

[32]   Simpson, op. cit., p. 42.

[33]   http://www.lsu.edu/visitors/history.shtml.

number of topics that covered not only the curriculum, but also the organization and management of KMI.

Sherman was seeking detailed information on "the exact price of each article of dress, and furniture furnished the cadets, price of each textbook—how supplied, cost of black-board, drawing board, mathematical instruments, drawing paper, paints, pencils." He also wanted to know what firm supplied the various items and if they were purchased wholesale and then sold to the cadets. In addition, were the cadets marched to the mess hall, and did they have regular reveille, tattoo, and taps? He also wanted information concerning uniform materials because he believed that the gray cloth used at West Point and VMI would not be suitable for wear in Louisiana.

A Young William T. Sherman—Young

Sherman was also concerned about the annual expense incurred by the cadets for clothing, mess hall, books, paper, lights, fire, washing, and tuition. He was aware that modifications might be necessary because of Louisiana's climate, but he felt that "this may all be done without in the least impairing that systematic discipline which I suppose it is the purpose to engraft on the usual course of scientific education." Shortly after his visit to Frankfort, Sherman left for Louisiana, where he would be joined on the Louisiana State Seminary of Learning faculty by David F. Boyd. In March, 1860, the name of the school was changed to Louisiana State Seminary of Learning and Military Academy. The school opened with five professors and nineteen cadets but would eventually have seventy-three students.[34]

After the outbreak of the Civil War on April 12, 1861, there was a wholesale exodus of cadets from KMI. Tension had been growing among the cadets during the presidential campaign leading up to the election of

---

[34] William T. Sherman to G. Mason Graham, September 7, 1859 in Walter L. Fleming (ed.) *General W. T. Sherman As College President*, Cleveland, The Arthur H. Clark Co., 1912, pp. 37-38; http://www.lsu.edu/visitors/history.shtml.

Abraham Lincoln and tempers had occasionally boiled over. William Simpson cites one instance of a number of fistfights that broke out during dinner. Within a few short weeks, there were only a few cadets and faculty members still present at the school.[35] It is impossible to determine exactly

how many cadets actually served during the war. James Stephens, who did extensive research in the *Official Records of the War of the Rebellion* for his *Reflections*, could only compile a list of those killed during the war. Stephens listed fifty-three former cadets killed in the service of the Confederate

Old Barracks at Frankfort—Venice

States and twelve in the service of the United States.[36] William Simpson states simply that "Kentucky Military Institute furnished scores of soldiers to both armies. These former cadets were without exception officers. Their rank ranged from lieutenant to Major General."[37]

One story growing out of the Civil War concerns John Hunt Morgan, the famous Confederate Cavalry commander. Many sources maintain that Morgan attended KMI, which is wrong. What may have caused the confusion was that a cadet named J. H. Morgan, who was from Mississippi, graduated from KMI in 1861. In addition, two of John Hunt Morgan's brothers attended KMI, Richard Curd Morgan, who graduated in 1852, and Thomas Hunt Morgan, who attended for one year.[38]

One KMI graduate who served in the United States Army during the Civil War was the recipient of the Medal of Honor. Henry V. Boynton was an 1859 graduate who served in the 35th Ohio Infantry throughout the war. He received the Medal of Honor for his actions during the Battle of Missionary Ridge, Tennessee, where he continued to lead his men after being severely wounded. While a student at KMI, he was a member of Phi Delta Theta fraternity. After the Civil War, he was a newspaper

---

[35] Simpson, op. cit., p. 46.
[36] Stephens, op. cit., p. 301.
[37] Simpson, op. cit., pp. 46-47.
[38] Stephens, op. cit., p. 61.

correspondent and was chairman of the committee that oversaw the development of the Chattanooga National Military Park.[39]

The most successful former KMI cadet in the Civil War was Robert F. Hoke of North Carolina. Hoke was enrolled by his widowed mother when she realized that he had advanced beyond the courses offered by the school in his hometown of Lincolnton. Hoke entered KMI in the fall of 1852 at the age of fifteen. While at KMI, Hoke studied Virgil, Latin, English, and American history. After one year, Hoke was forced to leave school and return home to help manage the family's extensive business holdings.

During the Civil War, he fought in most of the important battles in the eastern theater. He rose through the ranks from second lieutenant to major general. Following the war, Hoke returned to Lincolnton to once again manage his family's businesses. He would avoid politics and remained silent about his activities during the war. In his later years, he bore a striking, if not eerie, resemblance to Robert E. Lee. Hoke's fellow cadet, Leland Hathaway, wrote that "An able faculty made this one of the best and most thorough institutions in the United States. It ranked side by side for years with the Virginia Military Institute and other institutions of the first class. The military instruction and discipline were copied rigidly from that maintained at West Point."[40]

Although KMI ceased operations with the outbreak of the Civil War, Colonel Morgan retained ownership until August 17, 1863. Because his health was failing, Colonel Morgan sold the school to Burrell Bassett Sayre, a well-known teacher at the Frankfort Academy. The *Tri-Weekly Commonwealth* carried the following notice:

The Kentucky Military Institute was sold on Monday (August 17, 1863) to B.B. Sayre for $10,000. We are not advised as to what use it will be put, but have no doubt that it will be reopened as

General Robert F. Hoke—Young

---

[39] http://en.wikipedia.org/wiki/Henry_V._Boynton.

[40] Barefoot, Daniel W., *General Robert F. Hoke: Lee's Modest Warrior*, Winston-Salem, John F. Blair, Publisher, 2001, pp. 15-16.

a school under the auspices of Mr. Sayre. He is the most successful teacher in America.[41]

Mr. Sayre did not reopen the school until the end of the Civil War. The first session started on September 25, 1865. Although the military training was retained, Mr. Sayre felt that it was unwise to issue arms to the cadets and uniforms were not worn. The tuition for one semester was one $175. Despite the fact that Mr. Sayre reopened the school, his tenure was about to end.

---

[41]   Quoted in Simpson, op. cit., p. 52.

Chapter II

—◆—

THE ALLENS RETURN

In February of 1866, Colonel R. T. P. Allen returned to Frankfort from Texas and managed to regain control of the school. Although the details are unknown, he apparently purchased the school from Mr. Sayre. Where Colonel Allen obtained sufficient funds to buy the property is open to question. His grandson mentioned the fact that he was related to Jay Cooke as did his half niece, Katherine S. Forwood. It is possible that Cooke, perhaps the wealthiest man in the United States following the Civil War, was willing to assist his brother-in-law in his efforts to regain control of KMI.[42] It should be noted that one of the colonel's grandsons was named Jay Cooke Allen, perhaps an indication of the closeness of the relationship between the families. Colonel Allen retained the faculty that Mr. Sayre had assembled. Mr. Sayre returned to his independent teaching duties.

One unusual story from the Civil War concerns the fate of the Kentucky Chi Chapter of the Sigma Alpha Epsilon (SAE) fraternity. The Kentucky Chi Chapter had been founded at KMI in December 1860. The fraternity had been founded initially at the University of Alabama in 1856. By the time the Civil War began, there were fifteen chapters, fourteen of which were located at schools in Southern States, the other was in the District of Columbia. As students left KMI after hostilities

---

[42] John H. Allen to Col. C.B. Richmond, March 29, 1941; http://wc.rootsweb. ancestry.com/cgi-bin/igm.cgi?op=GET&db=black100/d=I16296; http://www.9key.com/markers/marker_detail.asp?atlas_number=5021009147.

began, the last two members of the fraternity tried to determine what to do with the chapter's secrets and documents.

John B. Kent and Bulow Ward Marston decided to ask Lucy Phenton Pattie, an eighteen-year-old girl who lived on a farm adjacent to the campus, if she would keep the secrets of the order. Lucy agreed to keep the secrets and not give them to anyone who did not give her the secret handshake. With the secrets safe, the two young men left to join the Confederate Army. Kent was killed at the Battle of Chickamauga, and Marston was wounded at the Battle of Shiloh and did not return to KMI after the war.

In 1868, a member of the SAE chapter at Washington College came to Farmdale and initiated six new members, one of whom was Colonel Allen. The colonel went to Lucy and ask for the secret orders, but she refused because the colonel did not use the secret handshake. It would be several months before another member of the Chi Chapter went to Lucy, greeted her with the handshake, and received the secret orders. A few months after the chapter was reorganized, the members offered Lucy a full membership in the fraternity. Colonel Allen, apparently impressed by the young woman, allowed Lucy and a friend, Helen L. Carmer, to attend classes at KMI.[43]

Although many members of Lucy's family are buried in a family cemetery located on the former KMI Farmdale property, Lucy is buried in the Frankfort Cemetery. Her original gravestone was replaced by one donated by the Kentucky Epsilon SAE Chapter. The stone has the inscription "This monument was erected in 1977 by Kentucky Epsilon SAE

Members of Sigma Alpha Epsilon
Fraternity—Venice

---

[43] Stephens, op. cit., 70-72; Jenny Thompson, "Lucy Phenton Pattie: 'A Brave Splendid Woman, This Daughter of SAE,'" *The Record: The Quarterly Journal of Sigma Alpha Epsilon*, Spring, 2004, http:// en.wikipedia.org/wiki/Sigma_Alpha_Epsilon, http://en.wikipedia.org/wiki/ list_of_Sigma_Alpha_Epsilon_chapters.

Chapter in honor of Sigma Alpha Epsilon's only woman member, Lucy Phenton Pattie."[44] It is interesting to note that the *Cadet Adjutant* included Ms. Lucy and her sister in the section "For the Old K.M.I. Boys."[45]

Following the Civil War, Meriwether Lewis Clark joined the KMI faculty as commandant of cadets and professor of higher mathematics. Clark was the son of William Clark, who, with Meriwether Lewis had explored the Louisiana Purchase Territory to the Pacific Ocean from 1803 to 1806. Clark graduated from West Point in 1830 and then served as a map maker during the Black Hawk War. He resigned from the army in 1833 and worked at various jobs, most notably as an architect. Clark saw service in the Mexican War and then returned to civilian life. One of his major achievements was designing the St. Vincent de Paul Roman Catholic Church in La Salle Park in St. Louis.

Clark served in various staff positions in the Confederate Army during the Civil War. Following the surrender of General Robert E. Lee at Appomattox, Clark returned to Louisville. He joined the faculty of KMI in 1866 and served for about three years. Following his time at KMI, he returned to his architectural work in which he designed a number of buildings in Frankfort and Louisville. Clark's son, Meriwether Lewis Jr., was responsible for founding the Louisville Jockey Club, the construction of Churchill Downs, and the running of the Kentucky Derby. [46]

During the 1866-1867 session, Colonel Allen made his two sons, Robert D. and John H. Allen his partners in the ownership of KMI. In 1874, when Colonel Allen retired, Robert D. took control of the school. There is little or no information about when John H. gave up his connection with the school. Three of John H's sons attended KMI: John H. Allen Jr., 1886; R. T. P. Allen Jr., 1865-1866; and Jay Cooke Allen, 1885-1886.

---

[44] Stephens, op. cit., 71, http://www.usgennet.org/usa/ky/county/franklin/indeex/pattiegraveyard.html.

[45] The *Cadet Adjutant*, Vol. XIV, No. 5, p. 2.

[46] Robert E. L. Krick, *Staff Officers in Gray: A Biographical Register of the Staff Officers in the Army of Northern Virginia*, Chapel Hill, University of North Carolina Press, 2003, p. 97, http://en.wikipedia.org/wiki/meriwether_lewis_clark,_sr., http://www.math.usma.edu/people/rickey/dms/00609-clark.htm, http://en.wikipedia.org/wiki/M._lewis_clark.

By the time he joined his father in the ownership of KMI, Robert D. had already led a varied life. He was born in Washington DC in 1836. He had graduated from KMI in 1852 and then attended Louisville University, where he obtained his medical degree in 1856. He joined his father at Bastrop Military Institute in Texas as a mathematics instructor. In 1858, he married Laura Sims, and they would have four children. One of their children, Robert Sims, would graduate from KMI in 1883. After he graduated, he was commissioned in the regular army. His first assignment was as tactical instructor and commandant at KMI. He eventually married his adopted sister, and they moved to Texas. When the Civil War began, Robert D. enlisted as a captain in the Seventeenth Texas Infantry. He resigned his commission because of ill health on August 26, 1863. Following the conclusion of the war, he returned to Kentucky with his father.[47]

Upon his return to KMI, Colonel R. T. P. Allen made only a few changes to the school's curriculum. He did add a very elementary course in medicine and a professional law course. The new courses were primarily open only to resident graduates. However, undergraduates could take the courses if the superintendent approved. Presumably, R. D. Allen would teach the medical course since he held a medical degree from Louisville University.[48] Colonel Allen did put the cadets back in uniforms and issued them rifles. He had anticipated some discipline problems because many of the cadets were veterans of the Civil War, but no problems developed. He assumed that the former soldiers, because of their military service, saw the value of discipline in their daily lives.

The first session after the Civil War saw more cadets enrolled than at any other time in the school's history. With an enrollment of 167 students, Colonel Allen considered the year a complete success. He believed that enrollment might have been better if more people in the South had known that the school had resumed operations.[49] Tuition for the school year was $350 a year; half of the amount was due at the beginning of the year and

---

[47] Stephens, op. cit., 99; http://0-www.tshaonline.org.sapl.sat.lib.tx.us/ handbook/online/articles/falah.

[48] Catalogue of the Kentucky Military Institute for 1867, Frankfort, Kentucky., S.I.M. Major Co., pp. 4-5.

[49] Ibid., pp. 23-24.

the second half due at the midpoint of the session. Uniform costs were additional and ranged between thirty and thirty-five dollars.[50]

On October 25, 1865, Colonel Allen's name appeared on a list of former Confederate civil and military leaders who had applied for a presidential pardon for their service during the Civil War. As a graduate of West Point who had served the Confederacy, Allen was ineligible for a pardon under the terms of President Johnson's first amnesty proclamation issued on May 29, 1865. By the end of 1867, President Johnson had issued more than 13,500 individual pardons and only about 300 former Confederates had not been pardoned.[51]

In 1867, enrollment again reached a new high with 177 students enrolled. In his history of the school, William Simpson notes a decided shift in the demography of the student body. Before the Civil War, a large number of cadets were from northern states. In 1867, only one cadet was not from a Southern state.[52]

The grading system for a number of years had been on a scale of zero to ten. The grade of 0 indicated utter ignorance while 10 indicated a thorough knowledge of the subject. Each student received a grade each day in each subject.[53]

One of the students who entered KMI following the Civil War was William Harding Carter. He began his service in the Union Army as a dispatch rider at the age of twelve. Following the Civil War, he completed his schooling in Nashville, Tennessee and then entered KMI. He graduated in 1869 and, at the age of seventeen, went to attend West Point. Upon graduation, he was assigned to the Eighth U.S. Infantry, but he would transfer to the Sixth Cavalry. Carter would be the recipient of the Medal of Honor "for distinguished bravery in action against the Apache Indians."

---

[50] Ibid., p. 29.

[51] *New York Times*, "Applicants for Pardon: List of all the High Military and Civil Rebel Leaders now Suing for Pardon," http://www.nytimes.com/1865/10/25/news/applicants-for-pardon-list-all-high-military-civil-rebel-leaders-now-suing-for.html; http://www.tngenweb.org/civilwar/pardons/center.html.

[52] Simpson, op. cit., 63. The one cadet not from a southern state was from Illinois,. Catalogue of the Kentucky Military Institute for 1868, Frankfort, Kentucky., S.I.M. Major Co., 1968, p. 23.

[53] Catalogue of the Kentucky Military Institute for 1868, p. 15.

Carter's later work with Secretary of War Elihu Root to reform the army in the early twentieth century was extremely important. The two men are credited with the creation of the Army War College and helping to pass the General Staff Act of 1903. Carter also worked in support of the Militia Act of 1903, which proposed replacing the obsolete state militias with the National Guard Bureau.[54]

On February 11, 1868, the *Daily Kentucky Yeoman* published an article that praised KMI and predicted that as the South's economy recovered, the school would continue to grow:

> Among the institutions of the State in which our citizens should feel a commendable pride is the Kentucky Military Institute located in the vicinity of this city. About 170 pupils have matriculated this year; and although at the close of the last term, a number from the South were necessitated to withdraw, from the inability of their parents, in the impoverished condition of their section, to pay the fees of the Institution, the Corps of Cadets is larger at this date than at any other period of its history. Could the South recover from her financial prostration, the buildings would have to be enlarged to accommodate the pupils who would flock to the Institute from that quarter.[55]

In 1855, the faculty and students had started publishing a school newspaper called the *Institute Pet*. The name was quickly changed to *Kentucky Military Institute Magazine* and would continue publication until the school closed with the beginning of the Civil War. William Simpson states that KMI was the first school to successfully support a school magazine. Following the reopening of the school in 1866, publication of the magazine resumed. After only one year, the magazine failed for lack of financial support. Publication of the magazine resumed again in 1870. The content of the magazine was devoted to short stories, poems, and articles written by cadets.[56]

---

[54] http://en.wikipedia.org/wiki/William_Harding _Carter and Ronald G. Machoian *William Harding Carter and the American Army, A Soldier's Story.*

[55] Quoted in Simpson, op. cit., p. 64.

[56] Simpson, op. cit., pp. 71-74.

In the spring of 1867, the president of the KMI Board of Visitors, Kentucky adjutant general D. W. Lindsey, requested that Governor Thomas Bramlette supply new rifles to the school. Many of the school's rifles had been taken back by the state during the Civil War for issue to state troops. Following the war, the cadets were left with a mixture of old Springfield muskets and Austrian rifles.[57]

It would be four years before new rifles arrived at KMI. The rifles were model 1866 cadet Springfield rifles made specifically for use at the United States Military Academy, universities, and state schools that had military training courses. The rifles had shorter barrels and thinner stocks to reduce the weight of the weapon. Approximately four hundred of the cadet rifles were shipped to the state of Kentucky, of which one hundred would be issued to KMI for use by the cadets.

One of the cadet rifles would find its way to the Smithsonian Institute in 1912. The rifle is significant because "it is a very early cadet breach loading rifle, having been among the first 424 cadet Trapdoor rifles made." In cleaning and repairing the rifle after it was shipped from Rock Island Arsenal, the Smithsonian technicians found three notes in a hole concealed by the butt plate. The notes were written by three cadets who had used the rifle between 1881 and 1883. It is unclear how long the rifles were used by the school, but it was probably until the end of the century.[58]

There were a number of literary societies formed during KMI's history. In general, the societies met weekly for discussions, speeches, and refreshments. Each of the societies elected their own officers, and a faculty member served as a critic and advisor. During the meetings, each of the societies had dedicated rooms in which they met. The members learned the fine arts of debating and public speaking. The oldest of the societies was the Philomathean Society, which was founded in 1848. The society, like KMI, held a charter from the Commonwealth of Kentucky. Membership in the society was by invitation only. The second oldest society was the Addisonian Society, which was founded in 1851 to compete with the Philomathean Society. Throughout its history, the Philomathean's had the reputation for having the best programs of all the societies. Its membership

---

[57] Simpson, op. cit., p. 60.

[58] David Miller and Charles Pate, "An Identified Cadet Trapdoor Rifle of the Kentucky Military Institute," *Military Collector and Historian* (Journal of the Company of Military Historians), 62:4, Winter 2010.

was also by invitation only. A third society, the Ealeanbonda, was founded in 1852.

When KMI moved to Lyndon, the cadets decided that another society was needed that would be open to any cadet who was not a member of the other societies. Consequently, the Deinologian Society was formed to serve as a preparatory group for the other societies. Among all of the societies, it had the reputation as the most democratic of the three. In 1905, the Polymnian Society was formed. The new society, known as the Pollies, quickly became a rival to the older groups. Membership in the Pollies was also by invitation. In 1908, another society, Roll of Forum Society, was formed, but little or nothing is known about it. All of the literary societies would play an important role in preparing the cadets for the orations they had to deliver under Fowler's superintendence. By the 1920s, the old societies were gone, and each company had a society of its own.

In addition to the literary societies, three new fraternities were founded in the 1870s to join the Sigma Alpha Epsilon fraternity at KMI. The first was the Kentucky Mu Chapter of Alpha Tau Omega (ATO) that was established on March 10, 1870. The first ATO chapter was started at Virginia Military Institute in the hope that North and South might be reunited in brotherhood. The second fraternity was Pi Chapter of the Chi Phi Southern Order; the second national fraternity to bear the name Chi Phi began on April 25, 1872, at KMI. The Southern Order of Chi Phi had been founded at the University of North Carolina in 1858. A fourth fraternity, the Kentucky Beta Chapter of Phi Delta Theta was founded at KMI at some point. All four fraternities continued at KMI until the 1880s. Since they were secret organizations, there is little or no information concerning the fraternities or their activities. The SAEs ceased to function in 1887, the Chi Phi in 1883, and there is no information about when the ATO and Phi Delta Theta chapters became inactive. The fraternities were popular with the cadets; every member of the graduating class in 1872 was a member of either the ATO, SAE, or Chi Phi fraternities. [59]

One club that existed along with the literary societies and fraternities was the Ugly Club. The members of the club attempted to make themselves

---

[59]   http://en.wikipedia.org/wiki/Chi_Phi_fraternity;   http://en.wikipedia.org/wiki/Sigma_Alpha_Epsilon;   http://en.wikipedia.org/wiki/Alpha_Tau_Omega; http://www.phideltatheta.org.

as ugly as possible so that they would not be attractive to young ladies. The purpose of the club was clear: "The object of our Holy Order is to fortify ourselves against the contaminating influence of the fair sex as we have, even at this early day, sad experiences caused by the evils occurring from their association."[60] In addition to the social clubs, there were two baseball clubs in existence in 1871. However, they ceased to exist that year as the cadets seemed to have developed an interest in croquet rather than baseball.

Members of Alpha Tau Omega
Fraternity—Kaufmann

In 1871, emphasis was placed upon the practical application of the lessons learned in various classes. The students worked on such things as the design and building of bridges. Additionally, the senior students engaged in the design of railroads, such as laying out the routes, running curves, and leveling the land and roadbeds. The students were primarily interested in the application of the mathematics and science involved in these projects.[61]

The estimated cost of a year at KMI was calculated to be $500. Tuition and board were $350, while the cost of clothing, incidental expenses, and pocket money was estimated at $150. The number of cadets was limited to 150.[62] Colonel Allen estimated that the cost to construct the school's buildings and other facilities was more than $100,000.

Each cadet entering KMI was required to subscribe in the Matriculation Register to the following obligation: "I hereby engage to serve as a Cadet in the Kentucky Military Institute, to faithfully observe its regulations, and to obey the order of its constituted authorities, and to abstain from all

---

[60] Quoted in Simpson, op. cit., 75.

[61] Simpson, op. cit., p. 77.

[62] Catalogue of the Officers and Cadets of the Kentucky Military Institute from September 4, 1871 to June 6, 1872, Indianapolis Sentinel Printing Co., 1872, p. 27.

spirituous drinks, and from the keeping or using private weapons of any kind for the time for which I have entered."[63]

The Catalog for 1872 contains an extensive list of rules and regulations governing the lives of the cadets. It is probably no accident that the contents of the *Blue Book* written by Colonel Charles Fowler in the twentieth century resembled Colonel Allen's list of rules; Fowler was a freshman in 1872. The regulations specifically mentioned that dances would not be permitted because they "have been found to work injuriously, by interrupting the studies of the cadets."[64]

The general course of study offered in 1872 was not significantly different than the course in 1854. For the resident graduate course, there was an elementary course of medicine and a professional course of law. The courses in engineering covered a wide range of topics, such as railway and road engineering; bridge building; canal and hydraulic engineering; steam engines; warming and ventilating homes; lighting, watering, and draining towns; reclaiming, draining, and irrigating lands; bookkeeping; railroad, boat, and other freight accounts. These courses, as well as many others, were all designed to prepare the graduates for careers in a rapidly growing industrial economy. It is interesting to note that the school was still using Colonel Edmund Morgan's Parallel of the Orders of Architecture along with his drawings in the engineering course.[65]

Colonel Allen had implemented a system to reward cadets whose conduct had been exemplary during the year. "Cadets receiving no demerits during one academic year, receive a medal *of white metal*, with suitable inscription. This badge, worn the succeeding ear without demerit, entitles the wearer to a *silver medal*; and the latter, worn the succeeding year, confers upon the holder, if a member of the first class, a *gold medal*—the grand badge of honor for good conduct."[66]

When Colonel R. T. P. Allen retired in 1874 and Robert Allen became the sole superintendent, he began to make some changes in the school's curriculum. He placed all of the courses into specific departments: preparatory, mathematics, natural sciences, English, civil engineering, and commercial. He also made certain that the time necessary to earn a

---

[63] Catalogue, op. cit., p. 28.

[64] Catalogue, op. cit., p. 27.

[65] Catalogue, op. cit., p. 6.

[66] Catalogue, op. cit., p. 25.

bachelor's degree would be at least four years. In order for a senior to graduate, he had to pass a fifteen-hour oral examination at which all members of the faculty were present.[67]

The emphasis on practical application that had started a few years earlier was increased by the new superintendent. The lecture method of instruction was increasingly changed to one of practical application of the course material. Mathematics was taught through the use of

The Campus in 1872—Bender

both lectures and the continual application of mathematic principles. Ancient languages were taught through extensive reading programs, while modern languages were taught through the conversational method. In the natural science, engineering, and commercial departments, practical applications were used to illustrate the course materials.[68]

Colonel Robert Allen's method of instilling self-discipline in cadets was to draw out the individual's pride in himself. The cadet's pride and his high moral principles would cause him to exercise the greatest degree of self-discipline. His views would be more completely implemented by one of his former cadets, Charles W. Fowler, when he purchased KMI.[69]

In 1873, Colonel Robert Allen spelled out the advantages that KMI offered:

1. An absolute exemption from the multiplied evils and temptations of a city life.
2. A single family for all connected with the Institution, under strict military government.
3. A division of the classes into small sections, so that each student recites every day.

---

[67] A listing of the courses for each of these departments is given in Simpson, op. cit., pp. 83-85.

[68] Simpson, op. cit., 86.

[69] *Kentucadet*, Vol. XXX, No. 2, December 1954.

4. Expenditures under the control of the Superintendent, so as to guard against extravagance on the part of the student.[70]

In 1876, a group of forty men met in the KMI chapel and voted to form an alumni association. The group elected Colonel R. T. P. Allen as the first president of the association. The association would continue in one form or another until the school closed.[71]

In 1878, an anonymous donation provided scholarships for fifteen students who were unable to pay their own tuition. The students were to be men of high physical and intellectual capabilities. The donation stipulated that preference would be given to orphans and the sons of teachers and ministers.[72]

In 1879, the students and faculty began the publication of a newspaper known as the *KMI News*. The paper would be published for two years and received wide circulation among former students and friends of the school. In 1881, the *KMI News* contained a request that alumni submit the names of prospective students. The article indicated that the school hoped to obtain the names of five thousand young men. As an incentive to the alumni, anyone submitting forty names would receive a color print of the school.[73]

Colonel R. T. P. Allen was a man with a wide variety of interests and ideas. Between 1872 and 1886, he was granted nine patents for inventions related to steam engines, typewriters, and typesetting machines. One invention, the KMI Steam Engine, was

Members of the Faculty in 1885-1961
Saber, Venice

innovative enough to be described in the magazine *Scientific American*. Apparently, none of the inventions were groundbreaking enough to

---

70 Catalogue of the Kentucky Military Institute for 1873, Frankfort, Kentucky., S.I.M. Major Co., 1873, p. 32.

71 Simpson, op. cit., p. 87.

72 Simpson, op. cit., p. 89.

73 Simpson, op. cit., pp. 92-93.

earn the colonel any significant income. One of his inventions was a steam-powered wagon which he drove from Frankfort to Louisville. He wrecked the wagon on the return trip to Frankfort. One of his most interesting ventures was the construction of his home in Frankfort in the 1840s. The house is the earliest known example of a poured concrete house in Kentucky. Concrete was not commonly used for construction in the United States until almost the turn of the century. The concrete was durable and strong while it offered the advantage of being fireproof and easy to maintain.[74] The *Cadet Adjutant* in 1912 reported that people referred to Colonel Allen's home as Allen's Folly.

The *Cadet Adjutant* reported that Colonel Allen actually invented the Remington typewriter, but he lost a court battle over the patent rights for the invention. Colonel Allen's business sense was summarized as follows: "Unfortunately, Colonel Allen was more of a scientific than a commercial inventor; in other words his chief pleasure was in combining old principles into new forms, and in demonstrating by a working model, usually produced largely by his own hands, that he was right; but he lacked the business ability to push his inventions to commercial success."[75]

Despite being retired, Colonel Allen stayed up with events. In 1875, he wrote to *Scribner's Monthly Magazine* to correct an article they had published concerning a poem written by Edgar Allan Poe. The magazine had stated that Poe had written the poem after leaving West Point in 1829. Allen pointed out that he and Poe had both entered West Point in 1830. Colonel Allen stated, "I remember him well. While at the Academy he published a small volume of poems which were not thought to have much

---

[74] "The KMI Steam Engine," *Scientific American*, Vol. XXIX, No. 22, November 29, 1873. Patent 129703, Jul 23, 1872, Improvement in Rotary Steam-Engines; Patent 130888, Aug 27, 1872, Improvement in Steam-Valves and Cut-Offs; Patent 137163, Mar 25, 1873, Improvement in Rotary Valves and Variable Cut-Offs; Patent 142660, Sep 9, 1873, Improvement in Steam-Engines; Patent 167726, Sep 14, 1875, Improvement in Type-Setting Machines; Patent 171335, Dec 21, 1875; Improvement in Type-Writing Machines; Patent 185714, Improvement in Type-Writers; Patent 195072, Sep 11, 1877, Improvement in Type-Distribution Machines; Patent 351559, Oct 26, 1886, Car-Starter (Streetcar); National Register of Historic Places Inventory, Nomination Form, Col. R. T. P. Allen House, July 10, 1979.

[75] The *Cadet Adjutant*, Vol. XIV, No. 3, August, 1912.

merit. He was too much occupied with his poetry to attend to the severe studies of the course at the Academy, and hence resigned, in order to devote his whole time to poetry." The colonel related that in 1834, he was told by an acquaintance that "Poe was then working in a brick-yard in Baltimore, being engaged in wheeling clay in a wheel-barrow."[76]

Colonel Allen was a dedicated educator and undoubtedly a highly motivated individual. However, his seeming inability to maintain his focus on a project for any extended length of time was probably a source of many of his financial problems. His half niece, Katherine S. Forwood, summed up the family's feelings about the colonel: "One of my mother's half-brothers was . . . Col. Robt. T. P. Allen (nicknamed Rearin', Tearin', Pitchin' Allen) a brilliant but erratic character who caused his relations many sorrowful hours by his misdirected talents."[77] On July 9, 1888, while visiting his grandson, John Howell Allen, KMI 1886, at his home at Kissimmee, Florida, Colonel Allen drowned in a fishing accident. He was buried in the family plot in the Greenwood Cemetery in Orlando, Florida.

Despite the fact that he owned a private school, Robert Allen worked for many years to improve and further public education in Kentucky. He was one of the organizers of the Kentucky State Teachers Association, which was a

Cadets Exercising in the 1880s-1952 Catalog

predecessor of the Kentucky Education Association. He had served as a member of the Kentucky State Board of Education from 1876 to 1880. In addition, he was the president of the Kentucky State Teachers Association from 1884 to 1887. In 1878, he had started a normal school at KMI for teachers who wished to further their education. Colonel Allen was selected by the State Board of Education to be the head of the school. Allen donated

---

[76] http://www.eapoe.org/papers/misc1851/18751101.htm; The poem was not published during Poe's lifetime. It was first published by Scribner's Magazine in 1875 and is now known as "Alone," a title not used by Poe.

[77] http://wc.rootsweb.ancestry.com/cgi-bin/igm.cgi?op=GET&db=black100/d=I16296. The Colonel had been given his nickname by the troops he trained during the Civil War.

the use of the school's facilities to the state, and the attendees only had to pay for their board. Upon completion of the course, the teachers were awarded a diploma which entitled them to teach in any common school in the state. After two years, the State withdrew its support for the program and it closed.[78]

Colonel Allen successfully operated KMI for a decade after his father retired. However, for reasons never fully explained, he began to acquire large debts beginning about 1884. In September 1884, an article appeared in the Louisville *Commercial* with the headline, "The KMI in a Bad Way." The article stated that enrollment had declined over the last two terms, and a number of faculty members had not been paid and were suing Colonel Allen. The drop in enrollment was attributed in part to the overall improvement of the Kentucky public school system. The article also said that the school had not been able to pay its expenses for the last two years. Additionally, it reported that there were only about twenty students enrolled. The situation was so bad that there were insufficient funds available to feed the few students in attendance. The writer speculated that the school would have to suspend operations very soon.

Colonel Allen was outraged by the article and wrote a rebuttal which was published by the *Commercial.* The colonel stated that there were more than forty students enrolled for the current term. He stated that the school was freer of debt than it had been for many years. All members of the faculty had been paid in full, and there were no law suits against the school or the superintendent. Additionally, he stated that there was no thought of suspending the school's operations, even for a short period. Colonel Allen indicated that for several years, there had been various attacks upon the school which had

Member of the Faculty, 1888-1961
Saber—Venice

---

[78] The *Kentucadet*, Vol. XXX, No. 2, December, 1954, p. 5; Simpson, op. cit., p. 94; William E. Ellis, *A History of Education in Kentucky*, Lexington, University of Kentucky Press, 2011.

seriously damaged its ability to recruit students. He predicted that the school would survive all of the attacks being made against it.[79]

Whatever the actual financial situation had been in 1884, by 1887, Colonel Allen's financial problems were serious enough that he was forced to sell KMI to the Frankfort merchants Crutcher and Starks. The firm had sold uniforms and other supplies to the school, and presumably, Allen owed them money. The price paid for the school was the amount of the mortgage held by the Farmer's Bank of Frankfort. After he sold the school, Colonel Allen and his wife moved to Louisville. Apparently, his credit was sufficient to allow him to purchase a piece of property and open the Louisville Military Academy. Just as he had done at KMI, Allen conducted a summer school for teachers at the Louisville school. Little is known about Allen's activities in Louisville. He would eventually close the school and move to Texas, where his health failed as did his financial dealings. Colonel Allen died in Houston, Texas on May 6, 1913.[80]

Colonel Allen left the school in serious financial trouble. A member of the Class of 1885, J. W. Gaines, who at been a cadet when Allen was the superintendent, said, "Colonel Allen was one of the greatest teachers I have ever known. He could make mathematics become a live subject full of meaning and understanding to all who listened; but, unfortunately, he was not a business man."[81] KMI was closed for one year, 1887-1888, while the stock

Cadets, 1885—Venice

---

[79]   Stephens, op. cit., pp. 17-18; Simpson, op. cit., pp. 96-97. Simpson dates the controversy in 1887.

[80]   Simpson, op. cit., pp. 97-98; Stephens, op. cit. pp. 18-19; The *Kentucadet*, Vol. XXX, No. 2, December, 1954, http://0-www.tshaonline.org.sapl.sat.lib. tx.us/handbook/online/articles/falah. Simpson says that Allen died in 1909 as does the article in the *Kentucadet*. Stephens says he died sometime after 1909. The biography from the Texas State Historical Association gives the 1913 date.

[81]   The *Kentucadet*, Vol. XXX, No. 2, December, 1954, p. 5.

company that leased the property from Crutcher and Starks searched for a new superintendent.[82]

Colonel David French Boyd was hired as the new superintendent of KMI effective in June of 1888. Boyd seemed to be extremely well qualified for the position. He had been on the faculty of the Louisiana State Seminary of Learning and Military Academy with William T. Sherman. When Louisiana seceded from the Union, Sherman resigned as superintendent and tried to persuade Boyd to join the Union Army. Boyd, a native of Virginia, chose to join the Ninth Louisiana Infantry, a part of the famous Louisiana Tigers of the Army of Northern Virginia. He later transferred to the Western Theater as an engineer. He was captured by Jayhawk militia and sold to the Union Army for $100. He was exchanged and returned to the South, largely because of the intervention on his behalf by General Sherman. Following the Civil War, he returned to the Louisiana Seminary of Learning and Military Academy. Following a fire in October of 1869, the seminary moved from Pineville to Baton Rouge and reopened in November of the same year.[83]

Boyd essentially wrote the Charter for Louisiana State University when the state legislature re-designated the Louisiana Seminary of Learning and Military Academy in 1870. In 1880, Boyd was accused of mismanagement of university funds and resigned as president. In 1883, Boyd became president of Alabama Agricultural and Mechanical College, which would eventually become Auburn University. He was cleared of any wrong doing at LSU and returned as president and professor of civil engineering in 1884. In 1888, he resigned as president and accepted the position as superintendent of KMI.

There is little or no information concerning the operation of KMI during Boyd's tenure as superintendent. All that is really known is that the number of students dropped, and by the time the school closed, there were only nine students, the colonel and one faculty member remaining at the school. It is not known if the fact that Robert Allen had opened his Louisville Military Academy had any impact on the enrollment at KMI. In 1890, the ownership of the school, including 150 acres, was transferred from Crutcher and Starks to a group of men representing KMI. The Boyd

---

[82]   Simpson, op. cit., p. 98.
[83]   http://www.lsu.edu/visitors/history.shtml.

papers in the LSU archives contain General Order No. 1, across the bottom of which Boyd wrote "Closed Forever." In the final morning report, the colonel noted that the session closed on June 15, 1893, at 7:30.[84]

When Colonel Boyd closed KMI, he took a teaching position at Ohio Military Institute, Germantown, Ohio. He was on the faculty there for a year before going to Michigan Military Academy, Orchard Lake, Michigan for three years. He would return to the faculty of Louisiana State University until his death on May 27, 1899.

Two of Colonel Boyd's sons attended KMI while he was superintendent. David French Boyd Jr. entered in 1891 and graduated in 1893. He was appointed to the United States Naval Academy from which he graduated in 1897. Following graduation, he was assigned as a naval cadet on the *USS Maine*. Boyd was aboard the Maine when it exploded in

David F. Boyd Hall—Louisiana State University—Young

Havana Harbor on February 15, 1898. Boyd was one of the 103 survivors of the explosion in which 260 crew members were either killed or missing. Boyd would spend the next thirty-four years in the navy, finally retiring as a captain in 1932. His brother, Leroy Stafford Boyd, attended KMI but did not graduate. Leroy would eventually become the assistant librarian at the Library of Congress.[85]

The closing of the school did not mean that the property would remain vacant and unused for very long.

---

84   Boyd Papers, LSU Archives; Simpson, op. cit., 103.

85   http://clanboyd.info/state/Louisiana/famhist/davidf/index.htm.

Chapter III

COLONEL FOWLER AND CHANGE

When word reached Mt. Sterling, Kentucky, that KMI would not open for the 1893 fall session, Charles W. Fowler was extremely interested in gaining control of the school. Fowler's parents had died when he was a young boy and his guardian had enrolled him at KMI. The young man was forced to drop out of school after only two years because his guardian had mismanaged his inheritance. Fowler returned to his home in Marietta, Ohio for two years. When he was sixteen, he returned to Frankfort and managed to convince Colonel R. D. Allen to readmit him to the school. In return for being allowed to attend KMI, Fowler agreed to teach at the school after graduation to pay the cost of his tuition.

Stewart School about 1900—Young

Fowler graduated in 1878 with a degree in civil engineering. For the next four years, he taught at the school until his debt to the school was satisfied. He then worked for several years as an engineer, but he was an educator at heart. For a few years he taught at various public schools in Kentucky. At some point during the late 1880s, he started his own school, the Kentucky Training School (KTS) in Mt. Sterling, Kentucky. The school was a military-type school, but several girls were admitted as day students.

It is entirely possible that Fowler would have purchased the Farmdale property when Boyd closed the school in 1893, but the creditors sold the property to Dr. John Quincy Adams Stewart, an 1847 KMI graduate, and his son, John P. Stewart, an 1892 KMI graduate. The doctor converted the property into what is now known as the Stewart Home School. The school is now under the direction of the fifth generation of the Stewart family, and it is a nationally recognized school specializing in the education of intellectually disabled students. Although Fowler did not obtain the Farmdale property, he managed to secure the KMI charter from the board of visitors.[86]

Fowler merged KMI and KTS at the Mt. Sterling location and adopted the KMI name. Because the school building was barely large enough to accommodate classrooms and administrative offices, the school operated as a day school. Almost immediately, Fowler began looking for a new location that would have the necessary space required to expand the school's facilities.

In his history of KMI, James Stephens identified seven women who attended KMI when Colonel Fowler merged his Kentucky Training School with KMI. The women were Carolyn Anderson, Minnie Duerson, Virginia Grubbs, Patricia Johnson, Ella Reid Prewitt, Harriet White, and Nell Winn. Stephens gives conflicting information when he states that Ms. Prewitt was the only female graduate of KMI in 1897. Later, he wrote that Virginia Grubb graduated in 1892 at Mt. Sterling, becoming the

first female graduate, and Ms. Prewitt was the second. Since Colonel Boyd did not cease operation of KMI at Farmdale until June of 1893, it is unclear how Ms. Grubb could have graduated from KMI in 1892 while attending the Kentucky Training School.[87] The *Kentucadet* reported that Mrs. Ella Reid Prewitt McCord died on February 22, 1955. The obituary stated that Ms.

Could These Be Six of the Seven Women Who Attended KMI?—Kaufmann

---

[86] http://www.stewarthome.com/about/history.

[87] Stephens, op. cit., p. 86.

Prewitt had come to Lyndon with Colonel Fowler and lived in his home while she completed her schooling.[88]

Fowler was an astute businessman and an excellent administrator, and he was convinced that moving the school to a location near Louisville would help in recruiting new students. In 1896, Fowler purchased ninety-six acres that had been a part of the Colonel Stephen Ormsby plantation. Judge Stephen Ormsby, a native of Ireland, came to Kentucky about 1784. In 1791, he was appointed judge of the Jefferson District Court and moved to Louisville. Ormsby served in Congress from 1811 to 1817, when he retired to his estate Maghera Glass, which means "green meadows" in Gaelic. In 1804, the judge's only son, Stephen Ormsby Jr., was born at Maghera Glass.

Legend has it that the judge wanted to build a large house on the property, but because of a superstition that if a man over fifty builds a new house, he will not live to occupy it, he had his son build the mansion. In 1830, the judge deeded the eight-hundred-acre estate to his son. The following year, Stephen Jr. married Martha Sherley. The couple had eleven children, all born at Maghera Glass. Judge Ormsby would die there in 1844. Stephen Ormsby would see service in the Mexican War with the Louisville Legion, first as a major, and then as a colonel. Colonel Ormsby died at the estate in 1869.[89] Little is known about the property following the colonel's death until it was purchased by Fowler. The property included the stately mansion, which would become known as Ormsby Hall, and a number of other smaller outbuildings. Kentucky Military Institute opened in Lyndon for the first time in the fall of 1896.

Major Fowler, his title at Mt. Sterling, was commissioned as a

Colonel Charles W. Fowler-Kaufmann

---

[88]   The *Kentucadet*, Vol. XXX, No. 4, May, 1955, p. 7.

[89]   Kentucky Historic Resources Inventory, http://genforum.geneology.com/cgi-bin/print.cgi?ormsby::704.html.

colonel on the governor's staff by Governor William Bradley. The title *colonel* would be used by all superintendents until Dr. Simpson became president in 1965. Colonel Fowler was probably the strictest disciplinarian of any of the superintendents, either before or after him. He developed two different sets of regulations to govern the conduct of the cadets. In 1909, he developed the Orders of Interior Discipline and Police, which was replaced by the Blue Book at a later date. Not only was Fowler a strict disciplinarian, he was also an innovator in his approach to educating young men. In addition, he drew upon his training as an engineer to develop numerous improvements to the school's facilities.

When the school opened in the fall of 1896, there were forty students enrolled. The cost of the session was $300 and included tuition, board, lights, fuel, and plain washing. There were additional costs for uniforms and other special items. Some of the students were day students because there was insufficient space to house all of the cadets on campus. Very quickly, a building program was started to expand the facilities in Lyndon. During the first year, a gymnasium was constructed, and two years later, the first barracks was built. The new facilities were not lavish. The cadets bathed in galvanized tubs, and the rooms were lighted by kerosene lamps. Colonel Fowler had correctly assumed that moving closer to Louisville would increase enrollment. By 1900, the size of the barracks had been increased by almost two-thirds to accommodate the increased number of cadets. In addition, a chapel, laboratory, bathrooms, and a steam heating plant were built. Finally, a water system with shower facilities and an electric light system were installed.

Enrollment continued to increase, and the construction of a second barracks was necessary in 1900. In addition, tennis courts, a bicycle, and running tracks were built along with baseball and football fields. The continued growth of the cadet corps and the expansion of the physical plant certainly justified Colonel

Graduating Class of 1900—Kaufmann

Fowler's decision to move the school to Lyndon. In 1910, Fowler remodeled the front of Ormsby Hall by extending the porch and adding the four large columns that still grace Ormsby Hall. At about the same time, a new gymnasium was constructed. [90]

The rooms in the old barracks on the Lyndon campus were almost Spartan; they were about ten-by-fifteen feet and were equipped with two single-folding iron beds with cotton mattresses. There was a table that was two feet wide and three feet long. In addition, there were two corner

Ormsby Hall and Barracks—Kaufmann

bookshelves, a washstand, a stationary wardrobe, an electric light, a water bucket, and a broom. All of the rooms were heated by steam from the school's heating plant. The cottages and tents that the cadets would occupy at Eau Gallie were furnished in a similar fashion.

The very sparse rooms were not unusual. In 1862, a Citadel cadet described his room as "a mirror, two small tables, a washstand, bucket, cup, wash pan, foot tub, wardrobe, four chairs, and a cot and mattress for each cadet." [91] Although some of the furnishings would change, cadets at KMI lived in similar conditions throughout most of the school's history. In the 1940s and '50s, a three-man room in the barracks in Lyndon contained a three-tiered bunk bed, three chairs, a long desk for three students, three dressers, and a closet. Only a few of the rooms had sinks. By comparison, the rooms in Venice, Florida were luxurious. The rooms had two single beds, a desk for two, two chairs, two dressers, and a private bathroom. Historian Jennifer Green states that Alden Partridge, the founder of the American Literary, Scientific, and Military Academy, the future Norwich University, in 1819, believed that "'living a Spartan life' bonded the cadets and erased external social distinctions."[92]

School Motto—Young

[90] Simpson, op. cit., p. 107.

[91] Green, *Military Education*, op. cit., p. 67.

[92] Green, *Military Education*, op. cit., p. 68.

The first motto of the school selected by Colonel Fowler was "An Aristocracy of Gentlemen." Perhaps using the definition of aristocracy used by Plato and Aristotle, government by those whose character best fits them for the task, Fowler hoped to instill a certain code of conduct among the cadets. The motto only lasted a few years until it was changed to "Character Makes the Man." The new motto more appropriately conveyed what Colonel Fowler hoped to accomplish, the education and training of men of good character.

In 1900, although it was located in Lyndon, the cadet corps was invited to Frankfort to participate as the honor guard in the inauguration of Governor John C. W. Beckham after the death of Governor William Gobel following his inauguration. Governor Gobel was shot by an assassin the day before he was sworn in as governor. His swearing in ceremony was conducted on his deathbed, and he died the following day.

At no time were KMI cadets allowed to be married, but at least one cadet was divorced. In 1904, the *New York Times* reported that eighteen-year-old Harry Blackburn eloped with Verna Blackburn in Blairville, Virginia, when he was fifteen. Apparently, the marriage lasted only about thirty minutes. Harry's father, described as a millionaire mine owner, immediately sent Harry off to KMI. All Harry knew about the divorce was that he signed some papers given to him by his father's attorney.[93] Cadet Blackburn graduated in 1905 after a distinguished career as a student and athlete. Considering Colonel Fowler's concern about a prospective cadet's conduct before coming to KMI, the admission of Blackburn appears a bit unusual. Perhaps the colonel was willing to overlook an impulsive act by a young boy.

KMI offered AB and BS degrees after Colonel Fowler moved the school to Lyndon. There were four courses of study that a student could pursue: the graduates of the

Corps Preparing for Governor's Inaugural Parade—Kaufmann

---

[93] "Boy Cadet Divorced," *The New York Times*, April 1904.

practical course and the university course were awarded AB degrees; graduates of the scientific course received the BS degrees; and the students who completed the commercial course, which was only two years long, received a diploma rather than a degree. Tuition in 1900 was $300; there was an extra charge for uniforms and other special fees.[94] After the move to Lyndon, KMI would increasingly become a college preparatory school. By 1913, it had been reduced to a preparatory school and the equivalent of a junior college.

There is no information about when Colonel Fowler made the decision to begin the experiment of taking the school to Florida. Most certainly, he had to have been considering the idea for some time and took the time necessary to find a suitable location for the new campus. Considering Fowler's belief in the value of an active outdoor life, leaving Kentucky during the winter months was not surprising. The site he selected was a plot of about fourteen acres located on the Eau Gallie River, just about a half mile above where it joined the Indian River on the east coast of Florida. The site had originally been developed as a resort, constructed, and furnished for $60,000, but it had only been used for a part of two seasons. The major structure on the property was the Hotel du Nil, which was refurbished and used as classrooms and barracks.[95] Colonel Fowler leased the property for a period of three years while he evaluated the experiment. The three years were so successful that Fowler purchased the property from William A. Warnock at the end of the lease on April 13, 1908.[96]

Little is known about Eau Gallie when KMI first came to town. A longtime resident, Raymond Irving, related that in the 1920s Eau Gallie was "a little town with dirt streets, cows roaming through the entire village, an abundance of palmettoes, and an ice plant

First Train to Eau Gallie—Morgan

---

94   Simpson, op. cit., p. 108.
95   *Melbourne A Century of Memories: The Melbourne Centennial Book*, Melbourne Area Chamber of Commerce Centennial Committee, 1980.
96   Abstract.

that also furnished electricity, no barber shop, and an ice wagon pulled by a horse that delivered big chunks of ice from house to house." There were two hotels in Eau Gallie. One was known as Military Inn, and after the arrival of KMI, was owned by William E. Horn. If Eau Gallie was "a little town with dirt streets" in 1920, one can only imagine what it must have been like when KMI first came to town in 1906.

In 1978, Irving, a longtime member of the Eau Gallie Black community, remembered going to work for Colonel Fowler shortly after World War I. He started work as a waiter in the KMI dining room and then went north with the school to become Fowler's chauffeur and butler. He remembered Colonel Fowler as "A fine person, a typical military man. He didn't smoke, drink or swear. The worst expression he ever used was 'ding it!'"[97]

Once he owned the property, Colonel Fowler began a program to improve the property that continued until he retired in 1919. The year following the acquisition of the facilities, an electric plant was constructed to supply power for lights. In addition, a bathhouse was build which utilized artesian sulfur water; a boat house was constructed, and all of the existing buildings were painted. In later years, the improvements would continue. Perhaps the most notable improvement was the construction of a swimming pool, which still exists today. The pool was made of cement and measured 30x52 feet with a depth ranging from four to six and a half feet. The pool was supplied with warm sulfur water from an artisan well that was 350 feet deep.[98]

Colonel Fowler explained the reason for the move to Eau Gallie in a short pamphlet "Describing A New Idea in Education." The colonel was firmly convinced that fresh air and sunshine were essential to good health and character. Consequently, the move to Florida was essential to avoid

New Swimming Pool at Eau Gallie—Kaufmann

---

[97] *Melbourne A Century of Memories*, pp. 79-80.
[98] Catalog 1914-1915, p. 92.

sickness among the students. He was delighted that the school had neither a hospital nor a nurse in residence to treat sick cadets. He believed that avoiding sickness was only a partial benefit, as he believed that it also "improved mental, moral and, and social conditions." Just as important was the improvement in the academic performance of the students during the time spent in Florida.

Colonel Fowler stated his firmly held opinion, echoed thirty years later by Colonel Richmond in the 1935-1936 catalog, that the sunshine and fresh air was essential to a good moral character. "All close observers know that the danger signal is set for a boy's morals in the winter season, when he is housed up without sufficient outdoor exercise and pure fresh air and sunshine; the cause is removed by spending the winter in Florida, where practically the whole time is passed outdoors, and at night sleeping with windows and doors wide open. The moral gain alone is worth the extra cost of the trip."[99]

Did Colonel Fowler Advocate This Much Exposure to the Sun?—Young

Colonel Fowler was especially pleased with the appearance of the cadets after their stay in Florida. "And it is perfectly safe to say that no other school can show such a healthy looking lot of boys." The colonel then made an interesting claim: "They cure consumption these days by plenty of fresh air and sunshine; why not present the possibility in your son's case by letting him live outdoors with us for a few years?" The colonel was quick to point out that KMI did not take boys with tuberculosis. However, he was convinced that boys with colds, coughs, and even pneumonia might be cured by the stay in Florida. Concerning the cost of tuition, the pamphlet stated that "considering what we give, our charges are absurdly low." The low charges were made possible by a number of factors:

---

[99]   C. W. Fowler, "Describing A New Idea in Education," p. 4.

1. We own our Kentucky property, consisting of ninety-six acres of bluegrass land and the necessary buildings. On the land we raise quite a large part of our supplies, some of which we carry to Florida.
2. We own our Florida property, consisting of fourteen acres of land and eleven buildings, well equipped for our purpose.
3. All supplies are cheaper in Louisville than in any Northern city.
4. We make our electric light, have our own water works (artesian sulfur well in Florida), heat by steam with cheap coal in Kentucky, and have cheap labor.
5. Neither rent, interest, nor dividends to pay.[100]

Contained within the booklet was a sales pitch to parents to visit the school during the winter.

Although there was no room within the school buildings for parents, there were reasonably priced accommodations in the Eau Gallie area. Recreational facilities, such as boating and fishing, were readily available at good rates. The only request that Colonel Fowler made was, "do not expect us to suspend our rules for your boy. Nothing is more detrimental to the discipline of a school than allowing a boy special privileges because his parents happen to visit the school or its neighborhood; and a school without discipline is no school at all, and unworthy of your patronage." The information concerning the Florida experiment would be included as a part of the general catalog in later years.[101]

The first movement of KMI from Lyndon to Eau Gallie must have been a time of great anticipation for Colonel Fowler and the school administration. At the same time, they undoubtedly were filled with a significant amount of apprehension. The move was without precedent. No school

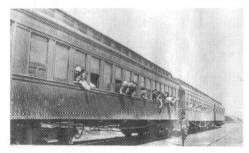

Train to Eau Gallie—Kaufmann

---

100 C. W. Fowler, "Kentucky Military Institute Winter Home," p. 11.
101 Fowler, "Describing A New Idea in Education."

had ever packed up its students, faculty, and staff and moved from one state to another, with the intention of reversing the move three months later. The cadets, faculty, and staff as well as all of the school equipment that would be needed in Florida were loaded aboard a special train in Lyndon. There are unconfirmed reports that the school's horses also made the trip to Florida. Undoubtedly, the cadets greeted the move with great anticipation and enthusiasm. They were setting off on a great adventure; they were a part of an experiment that had never been tried before. Not only that, they were going to Florida for the winter.

There is virtually no firsthand information available about that first trip to Eau Gallie. There are pictures of cadets moving items from the train to locations around the campus, but the year of the photos is unknown. Undoubtedly, there were problems; but over the years, the move would become routine. Lessons would be learned, and those who had made the trip in previous years knew what to expect and acted accordingly.

The train trip to Eau Gallie and back to Lyndon, covering more than eleven hundred miles each way, was an adventure for the cadets. The train made stops along the route for meals and visits to tourist attractions. In some cases, the cadets marched from the train station to their

Cadets Wait to Unload the Special in Eau Gallie—Kaufmann

destination. At other times parades were given at public events. It is a fair assumption that these parades were viewed by Colonel Fowler as an excellent way to gain publicity for the school. The appearance of the cadets in their uniforms would have made a lasting impression on those who saw them. Undoubtedly, more than a few new cadets came to the school as a result of these public displays by the cadet corps.

Cadets Unload Equipment in Eau Gallie—Kaufmann

During the return trip to Kentucky in 1908, the cadets participated in two parades. The first was a street parade in Atlanta. After the parade, the battalion was presented to Governor Hoke Smith. The second parade was held in Knoxville, Tennessee, on a baseball field near the University of Tennessee. The 1908 *Saber* reported that the parade was witnessed by several thousand spectators. On other occasions, stops were made in St. Augustine and Chattanooga. In St. Augustine, the cadets toured the old city and put on a dress parade for the citizens. While in Chattanooga, the cadets toured the Civil War battlefield and the tourist attractions on Lookout Mountain.[102]

Throughout the years that KMI wintered in Eau Gallie, the cadets were actively involved in the social life of the community. In March 1907, the cadets traveled by special train to Palm Beach to participate in Kentucky Military Institute Day. The corps marched from the train station to a baseball field where they gave a drill and a dress parade. The

New York Times Society Page reported that attention was focused on "the young men of prominent Southern families who are students at the school." Once the day's activities were over, the cadets returned to Eau Gallie by train.[103] There were also numerous dances and other social events in which the cadets participated.

Cadet March through St. Augustine—Young

It is not surprising that the cadets enjoyed their stay in Eau Gallie. The weather was excellent, and the social calendar was full. Every Saturday evening in 1908, a dance was held by the New Rockledge and Indian River Hotels. The *Saber* of 1908 praised the abundance of pretty girls at the Rockledge. "Many a cadet has

Dance at the Hotel Royal Poinciana—Young

---

102   *Saber*, 1908, p. 82.

103   The *New York Times*, March 15, 1907.

lost his heart as he waltzed to the strains of the "Merry Widow" or strolled in the moonlight among the palms along the Indian River." On Washington's Birthday in 1908, the Eau Gallie Yacht Club held a ball at their club. The grand march began at 8:30, and dinner was served at 10:00. Following dinner, dancing continued until a late hour. It was reported that everyone wished that they could celebrate Washington's Birthday every day.[104] Raymond Irving remembered that the biggest celebration in Eau Gallie was always Washington's Birthday. He always cooked for the celebration and remembered cooking three thousand pounds of fish one year.[105]

Major General Count Tcherep Spiridovich

On March 20, 1908, the corps of cadets went by train to Palm Beach for a parade and a military ball held in their honor. The cadets were allowed leave during the morning to tour the town. At four o'clock, the battalion marched through town to the baseball park. The parade was witnessed by an estimated crowd of several thousand people. That evening, a military ball was held at the Hotel Royal Poinciana. The grand march was led by Major General Count Tcherep Spiridovich of Russia and Captain William Miller, the KMI professor of Military Science and Tactics. They were followed by the KMI officers and cadets with their partners for the evening. The galleries of the ballroom were filled with

Squad of Naval Cadets on the Eau Gallie River—Kaufmann

---

[104] *Saber*, 1908, p. 83.
[105] *Melbourne A Century of Memories*, p. 81.

spectators. "When it had ceased to be late and was beginning to be early, first call was heard throughout the building and the cadets reluctantly bade their fair partner's adieu and hastened off to their waiting special train."[106]

The 1908 *Saber* noted the establishment of a Glee Club by Major Ford. The club was apparently popular with the cadets, especially their performances during chapel. "Chapel exercises have been rendered less monotonous by the good singing of the fellows who are members and we owe them our thanks." [107]

The move to Florida gave Colonel Fowler the opportunity to begin a program of naval instruction. In 1908, nineteen cadets made up two squads of students who received instruction in subjects such as rowing, sailing, buoys, lights, and the uses and names of the various parts of ships. The instructor was Captain L. S. Wood, a former naval officer, who took a squad out in the institute cutter, the *Coloosa*, several times a week to practice the principles learned in the classroom.

The classes utilized the Eau Gallie and Indian rivers as their primary classroom. Colonel Fowler anticipated that the school would be granted a number of regulation cutters and other equipment, such as machine guns, by the Navy Department under the provisions of a law recently passed by Congress. Under the program, instructors would be detailed to the school from the regular navy. All of the students would be required to learn how to swim. According to the 1908 *Saber*, "Everything is as in the United States Navy." No other information has been found concerning the course. However, several pictures of young men in white sailors' uniforms were found in a 1921 cadet scrapbook.[108]

Cadet in Sailor's
Uniform—Beard

---

[106] *Saber*, 1908, p. 82.
[107] *Saber*, 1908, p. 93.
[108] *Saber*, 1908, p. 69.

The *Saber* also published a list of Ten Commandments to guide the cadets. As irreverent as the cadets might have been, there was a probably a certain amount of truth in the list.

1. I am C. W. Fowler, Superintendent, and there shall be none ahead of me.
2. Thou shalt not say "damn," lest thou be stuck for gross profanity.
3. Remember Sunday and don't forget dress parade.
4. Five days shalt thou bone and the sixth walk guard duty, but the seventh thou shalt parade before the vast multitude.
5. Honor the faculty and officers that thy hours may not be spent walking extra duty.
6. Thou shalt not smoke.
7. Thou shalt not commit suicide.
8. Thou shalt not steal, for it is a reportable offense.
9. Thou shalt not bear grudges against coms and non-coms.
10. Thou shalt not covet they fellow cadet's mark, nor his roommate, nor his credits, nor his rat, nor anything that is his.[109]

One policy that Colonel Fowler instituted was the requirement that each cadet write a letter to their parents on Sunday night. There were exceptions to the requirement, but for most of the cadets, it was a Sunday night ritual. The policy was continued by Colonel Richmond after he acquired the school. Parents were encouraged to contact the school if they did not receive the weekly letter. Those cadets who had seen their parents during the week were excused from writing a letter, but for most cadets, a letter home was required.

Colonel Fowler appears to have wanted complete control over the cadets once they entered KMI. "Unless you have the fullest confidence in your ability to train your son properly, please do not enter him, if you enter him you must leave the details of the management to our judgment; do not write your son he may do this or he may do that 'if Colonel doesn't object,' but refer all such matters directly to the Superintendent. You should select your boy's teacher with as much care as you select your family physician, and leave your boy's case just as unreservedly to him."

---

[109] *Saber*, 1908, p. 113.

The colonel encouraged parents to contact him, but with one reservation: "Parents will please send all their correspondence on business matters direct to the Superintendent: he is rather too old to have his letters inclosed in one of his pupils!"[110]

Colonel Fowler established the policy of having parents deposit money with the school for a weekly allowance. "There's great danger in providing your son with unlimited spending money. Put him on an allowance and let that allowance be given him by the Superintendent in weekly installments, dependent on good conduct. It will save you money, teach him economy, and improve his deportment. From twenty-five to fifty cents a week is ample while in Kentucky, and double that in Florida." He concluded with the pessimistic comment: "You won't do this, either."[111]

On May 28, 1913, a new classroom building was dedicated on the Lyndon campus. With the permission of the inventor, the building was named the Thos. A. Edison Science Building. Edison sent Fowler a letter suggesting a possible admonition to be placed in the building.

To the Cadets of the Kentucky Military Institute:

> You are here to prepare for the battle of life. The victor in this, as in other battles, is the one who thinks best and works hardest, and keeps at it all the time.

Colonel Fowler was justifiably proud of the new building. The basement was completely devoted to shop work. It had a complete set of tools necessary for instructing students in shop work, which was a requirement to be completed by all of the students. All of the numerous tools were powered by electric motors and were the latest models available.

The first floor had two modern laboratories and two classrooms. The chemistry laboratory was equipped with individual worktables, each of

Chemistry Laboratory in the Edison Science Building—Catalog 1915

---

[110] Catalog 1914-1915, p. 23.
[111] Catalog 1914-1915, p. 22.

which had running water, gas, and electricity. There was a special ventilation system to remove noxious gases from the room. It was noted that this was a special concern of the colonel since proper ventilation was his hobby. The physical laboratory was also completely equipped with the latest available equipment. The entire second floor, with the exception of a small recitation room, was a chapel which would accommodate almost four hundred people. The entire building was extremely well lighted and heated by steam. Although there would be major renovations over the years, the second floor would eventually be divided into classrooms. The Edison Science Building would be the primary classroom building until the construction of two new classroom buildings in the 1960s.[112]

The dedication of the Edison Science Building was reported in the *New York Times*. After a brief description of the new facility, a new course of instruction was described. A two-year course in agriculture had been introduced by Colonel Fowler. There is little information available about the content of the course except

Machine Shop in the Edison Science Building—Catalog 1915

what was contained in the article. The course "will cover the ordinary farming operations as found in the Middle States and which will be put into practice on its farm of ninety-six acres in Kentucky, and in the Winter time will be devoted to citrus culture and truck gardening on its Florida estate, where the school spends the Winter."[113] By 1914, a citrus grove had been developed at Eau Gallie which consisted of 150 grapefruit and more than 300 orange trees which supplied the needs of the school.[114] Whether all cadets would be required to take the course or only those planning to operate a farm upon graduation was not made clear.

Colonel Fowler was adamant that only non-scholarship athletes should represent KMI. He considered those who received a reduction in tuition or were allowed to work for tuition to be professional or semiprofessional

---

[112] Catalog 1914-1915, p. 13 and Catalog 1935-1936, p. 31.
[113] The *New York Times*, May 28, 1913.
[114] Catalog 1914-1915, p. 92.

athletes. "No one is allowed to represent our school on the athletic field expect regular bona fide students, who are paying the regular tuition in cash, as stated in this catalogue." The colonel stated that the school received numerous applications seeking that regular charges be reduced, something he had no time to consider.[115]

Colonel Fowler was certain that the system he had put in place at KMI was far superior to a boy being raised by his parents and educated in public schools. "Parents usually make a great mistake in keeping their boys at home too long. No boy who is to be properly educated should be kept at home after he is fourteen years old, and most of them should be sent away before that time."[116] Despite believing that boys should be sent away to school at an early age, KMI did not admit boys younger than fourteen, unless a relative was also a cadet.[117]

Fowler was convinced that parents, because they loved their sons, would spoil them and not discipline them when it was needed. Additionally, he felt that many students who came to KMI had been poorly taught in their previous schools. He believed that it was possible to overcome both of these problems if the boy was enrolled soon enough. However, he cautioned that the parents should not expect too much:

> It is not every boy that will make a lawyer, doctor or other professional man. If you want to make a success out of your boy, educate him along the line of least resistance. Cultivate his natural gifts instead of trying to force an artificial growth. Remember, too, that we can only develop the "raw material" that you send us. Finally, do not expect marked results in a short time. You have had him fifteen years, more or less; what have you done for him in that time that is remarkable?[118]

Under the heading "A Few Ideas About Boys," Colonel Fowler discussed what he believed was the fundamental purpose of KMI:

---

[115]   Catalog 1914-1915, p. 32.
[116]   Catalog of 1914-1915, p. 20.
[117]   Catalog 1914-1915, p. 94.
[118]   Catalog 1914-1915, p. 22.

The average boy in his development passes through the same phases as the human race in its evolution; this being a fact, must be considered in his education. We accept only boys of good moral character, boys whose home influences have been elevating, and try to bring out the good there is in them and to repress the evil. To do this successfully no two boys require exactly the same treatment, but to determine just what this treatment should be requires the greatest skill, patience and labor. Parents could aid us wonderfully if they would only be more communicative in regard to the faults of their boys, so well as to their good points. Our object is to train the whole boy—soul, mind, and body; to do this we must have the most active and positive interest in your boy. The interest must not be spasmodic, as it is in those schools where the boy lives outside the college walls, and only appears at recitations, but it must be excited all the time, hence he should live in the family with his teachers. When a boy finishes our course successfully he is well prepared for life, for business, or for university work.[119]

Colonel Fowler believed that character was the most important trait that could be instilled in his students. He had adopted a new motto for the school, and he spelled out his idea of what "character" meant:

The only real use for a boy is to make a man out of him. To do this requires the utmost patience and skill, except in those very rare cases where the boy makes a man of himself, or perhaps it would be stating the case better to say it requires the best skill and talent on the part of the teacher to induce a boy to make a man out of himself; for nothing can be gotten out of him unless it is already there. In order to afford ourselves the best opportunities for success, we limit our number so that we may learn each boy; that we are ready to teach him. CHARACTER is our first aim, and we recognize that we can only form it, not create it; to do this requires the personal watch-care of teacher and parent. The parent is often too busy

---

[119] Catalog 1914-1915, p. 15.

to give his son the attention he should have, hence the necessity
of a conscientious, skillful teacher. We prefer to receive boys at
an early age, for they are then more receptive, and there is less
to undo; but boys under fourteen are not received, unless with
an older relative.[120]

Colonel Fowler felt that education should be a comprehensive
experience, and a student at KMI would be immersed in the overall
process;

> An Education with us means the symmetrical development
> of soul, mind and body; any one of these being neglected
> makes an unfinished man. The most dangerous men to society
> are educated men whose moral character is deformed, either
> by nature, which is very rare, we believe, or by neglect of early
> training. A successful experience for more than twenty-five years
> warrants us in claiming exceptional results in this direction. In
> mental training we seek to give the mind power rather than
> attempt to store it with information, believing that the power
> to know is better knowing; yet our course is more practical
> than that of most schools, as a comparison will quickly show.
> Our course of study is the result of our past experience and a
> careful study of some of the best schools in the Union.
>
> Believing that a text-book on morals does not meet the case, we strive to inculcate proper rules of action at all times.
>
> Recitations are but daily affairs, and they are so considered, character is for a life time, and its influence on others is

Members of the Philomathean Society
in 1908—*Saber* 1908

---

[120]   Catalog 1914-1915, pp. 15-16.

for eternity; hence the life here is made to bear as directly as possible on the boy's future.[121]

Colonel Fowler was determined to produce useful citizens, not just graduates. He stated that "Our ambition is to turn out capable men—rather than graduates." He continued to hammer home the point: "Our diplomas are certificates of working capacity, and we shall try to avoid the too often just criticism of 'helpless college graduates.' The fact that a boy is in the senior class is not conclusive evidence that he will obtain a diploma. Our work is practical if it is anything—we aim to give a breadth of grasp rather than mastering of detail."[122]

All candidates for graduation had to meet several requirements: (1) They were required to give five orations during the year. Four of the orations could be given either in chapel or one of the literary societies, but one had to be delivered commencement week; (2) all papers had to be written in good English. Any paper graded at less than seventy-five on the English had to be rewritten or be rejected entirely; (3) the candidates for a diploma had to pass written examinations in all subject in their course of study with a grade of seventy-five percent; (4) no cadet could graduate who had completed less than two years at KMI.

An example of the types of orations given by the seniors is shown by the topics covered at the 1916 Commencement. As a part of the declamation contest, the topics were the following: The Power of Public Opinion, Betsy and I Are Out, Political Conservatism, America's Mission, A Plea for Cuba, and How He Saved Saint Michael's. The issues covered in the speeches given during the Oration Contest were the following: Tendencies; Public Opinion; Are We civilized?; Preparedness; A Plea for Intervention in Mexico. Also, there was a debate between the Polymnian Literary Society, for the affirmative, and the Philomathean Literary Society, for the negative. "Resolved: That No Bill Now before

Members of the Polymnian Society in 1908—*Saber* 1908

---

[121] Catalog of 1914-1915, p. 16.

[122] Catalog of 1914-1915, p. 34.

Congress Provides for Adequate National Defense." All of these speeches and the debate were a part of the Commencement Week activities.

For undergraduate students, all examinations were written and given at the end of the quarter. Those students who had received a BA or BS degree could take another year of courses, after completing a thesis they would be awarded an MA degree. The postgraduate students were classified as cadet assistants, and their tuition was reduced from $400 to $300 for the year.

There were a number of different courses a cadet could choose from depending upon his goal in life. Depending upon what courses he took his senior year, he might be awarded a diploma as Graduate of KMI or a BS degree. There was the practical course, which was for the student who did not plan on attending a university. The scientific course prepared the student to enter the best technical university. Again, the course of study a student followed his senior year, he might be awarded a diploma as Graduate of KMI or a BS degree. The technical course, which was taken in conjunction with either the practical or scientific course, was another option. The university preparatory course was especially designed for students who expected to go to college. They were awarded a diploma as Graduate of the KMI. The commercial course was for those students who could not afford the expense of several years in college.

All of the students, except those enrolled in the university course, had some exposure to shop work and mechanical drawing. In 1915, the technical work consisted of a two-year course of study that would eventually be expanded to four years. The first two years of work would be bench work in wood, pattern making and turning, and probably chipping and filing. One fascinating feature of the wood-working class was that the student constructed a boat while in Florida.

Once the school returned to Kentucky, the students would be taught to use the turning lathe. When the lathe was mastered, the students would move on to pattern making. They would learn to construct "simple wooden patterns, the draft, shrinkage, and finish, molding in sand, the core, and finally the cast." The patterns that the students made would be used later in the foundry and machine shop.

The students also learned the principles behind the

Surveying Class—Kaufmann

operation of various types of gasoline engines. The school owned a variety of four-cycle and two-cycle engines ranging from two to fifty horsepower. The engines were from one to four cylinders and were both air and water cooled. Once the cadets had completed their work, they moved on to the machine shop. In the machine shop, the cadets were taught chipping, filing, fitting, and finishing so they could work with the items cast in the school's foundry. Instruction would follow in the use of lathes, drill presses, milling machines, and other tools. The end result would be the production of a tool or machine for the school. Such items as gas and steam engines, motors, dynamos, and machine tools were to be made.

Colonel Fowler believed that the technical work was extremely important to a cadet's education:

> It is not our desire nor intention to teach trades, but we do expect to teach a boy the theoretical and practical use of a great many tools, and the fundamental principles underlying many of the world's great industries . . . When a boy sees definite, practical results from his studies, it will no longer be necessary to reward or penalize him in order to get him to study.[123]

Following the outbreak of World War I in Europe, a preparedness movement, led by former president Theodore Roosevelt, General Leonard Wood, and former secretary of war Elihu Root, advocated military training in order to bolster the military preparedness of the United States. The movement resulted in the Plattsburg Movement, a series of training camps held at Plattsburg, New York, in which more than forty thousand young men were trained in 1915 and 1916.

On August 6, 1916, the *New York Times* published a letter from Colonel Fowler. "Should our Schoolboys Receive Military Training?" clearly stated Fowler's views concerning the value of a military education. The colonel pointed out that the public mistakenly believed that military training and militarism were synonymous. He argued that "doing the right thing, at the right time and in the right way, is the very foundation stone of success, and no school but a military school can successfully accomplish this work."

---

[123]   KMI Catalog 1914-1915.

Fowler argued that existing military schools were already producing individuals capable of becoming officers. "Schools like this are turning out material for officers every year, and everyone knows that the main difficulty in training an army out of raw material is to find proper officers to train the recruits." He continued, "The military training, as given in all well-organized military schools, not only in no way interferes with a boy's studies, but it actually adds to his efficiency, because of the economy of time due to its schedule of both work and play being rigidly adhered to."[124]

Sometime in 1916, a fire swept through a number of the cottages and buildings on the Eau Gallie campus. Colonel Fowler very quickly had the buildings replaced with new cottages. There is no mention of this fire in the various school records that have been discovered. However, there are a number of photographs of the damaged and destroyed cottages in the scrapbooks prepared by students during this time frame. Whether or

Fire-damaged Cottage—Beard

not the fire occurred when the school was in Eau Gallie is open to question. Since the colonel quickly had new cottages built and the cadets had photographs of the damaged buildings, it is possible that the fire happened when the cadets were in Florida.

Always an innovator and salesman, Colonel Fowler was constantly looking for ways to publicize his school. In an effort to reach parents and prospective students who might not be able to visit the school, he had two movies

Cottages at Eau Gallie—Beard

---

124 "Should our Schoolboys Receive Military Training?" The *New York Times*, August 6, 1916.

produced that illustrated student life at KMI. An advertisement that appeared in *A Handbook of the Best Private Schools of the United States and Canada* stated that anyone interested in the school could request copies of the films in order to assess the advantages offered by the school. At the time of the advertisement, there were thirteen faculty members, and the tuition was $500.[125]

The opening of school in 1918 found the cadet corps under a temporary organization. The temporary arrangement was necessitated by the problems caused by the influenza epidemic and the number of Old Boys eligible for commissions. KMI appears to have escaped the ravages of the epidemic that swept around the world from 1918 to 1920 and killed more than five hundred thousand people in the United States. Only one cadet was listed as having died as a result of the epidemic. Although the school had lost a number of cadets between the ages of eighteen and twenty to the draft, others who had enlisted without being drafted, and still others who had joined the Student's Army Training Corps (SATC) at universities, the school was filled to capacity.

One KMI graduate who served with distinction during World War I was Hugh Rodman. He was born at Frankfort, Kentucky, and graduated from KMI in 1875. Following his graduation, he attended the United States Naval Academy from which he graduated in 1880. He married Elizabeth R. Sayre, the daughter of Burrell Bassett Sayre, former superintendent of KMI. During the Spanish American War, he served in the Pacific and was commended for his conduct during the Battle of Manila Bay. From 1898 until the United States entered World War I, Rodman served in a variety of jobs advancing steadily through the ranks. He was promoted to the rank of admiral in 1917 and served as commander, Battleship Division 9, Atlantic Fleet aboard his flagship, *New York*. Ordered to take his division to Europe, they joined the British Grand Fleet at Scapa Flow. Until the end of the war, Rodman commanded his division in the North Sea. For his service, King George V invested him as a knight commander of the Order of the Bath.

In July 1919, he became commander-in-chief, Pacific Fleet, a position he held until 1921. Upon reaching age sixty-four, he retired. Despite being

---

[125] *A Handbook of the Best Private Schools of the United States and Canada*, Porter E. Sargent, 1915, p. 494.

retired, he continued to serve the nation in various capacities. In 1937, for example, he was the navy's official representative at the coronation of King George VI. Two naval vessels were named for Rodman: the destroyer USS *Rodman* (DD-456) and the transport USS *Admiral Hugh Rodman* (AP-126). Additionally, the U.S. Naval Station in the Panama Canal Zone bore his name. The USS *Rodman* earned five battle stars during World War II. Admiral Rodman died on June 7, 1940.[126]

The enrollment for the 1917-1918 school year was high, and it forced the use of tents to house thirty-six cadets in Eau Gallie. In order to eliminate the use of tents the following year, the barracks was expanded by adding eighteen rooms to the existing barracks during 1918. With the addition of the new rooms, nine on each end of the building, the barracks stretched for more than three hundred feet. There was speculation that some of the cadets, despite the availability of the new rooms, would choose to live in the tents again. It was reported that the tents were not uncomfortable since they were floored and equipped with electric lights and could be opened to allow proper ventilation. Additionally, the tents might be used to house some of the students returning to school from the SATC program.

There is no information available concerning the number of former cadets who served in the military during World War I. James Stephens lists three former cadets who died during the war, only one of whom was killed in combat. A number of cadets participated in the Students Army Training

Cadets March to Chapel in Eau Gallie—Kaufmann

Corps, and undoubtedly, there were others who enlisted. A poster printed in 1918, entitled Roster, lists the names of 186 cadets. The cadet corps was divided into three companies and a signal corps. It is interesting that there was no band company listed.[127]

---

[126] http://en.wikipedia.org/wiki/hugh_rodman; http://www.history.navy.mil/danfs/r8/rodman.htm.

[127] Stephens, op. cit., p. 301, KMI Poster from 1918, in the possession of the author.

By 1919, the train trip to Florida had become a familiar routine to the cadets. After eating supper on campus, the cadets boarded the train at Military Park, Kentucky, for Military Park, Florida. They ate breakfast the next morning in Knoxville, Tennessee and took lunch along the route. Supper was eaten in Macon, Georgia. The next day, the train rolled through Florida until it reached Military Park in Eau Gallie. The *Listening Post* summed up the trip in a way that might have been echoed by numerous other cadets making the trip, whether to Eau Gallie or later to Venice. "The trip brings a spirit of comradeship and good feeling that nothing else could. All look forward to a pleasant winter in Florida and are glad to leave the cold behind them. Those who do not take the trip are unlucky indeed, for it is one of the most pleasant occasions of the year."[128]

One young lady who attended a number of the social events in Eau Gallie in 1918 and 1919 was Ms. Jean Faircloth. During the winter months, she lived with her aunt, Mrs. Marie Glenn, whose son, William Frank Glenn, attended KMI. One woman who knew her said, "Jean was always taking up for the unpopular boys at Kentucky Military Institute. Those are the ones she chose to dance with, to be friends with . . . She was a lovely dancer."[129]

What Confusion?—Kaufmann

Twenty years later, Ms. Faircloth would become the second wife of General Douglas MacArthur. Former cadet William Hemphill, who submitted the information to the *Kentucadet* in 1947, said, "She will be remembered by all from the lowest 'Rat' to the Senior Captain."[130] The *Listening Post* from 1919 lists Ms. Faircloth as an attendee at a number of dances and other social functions sponsored by the school. It would be

---

[128]   The *Listening Post*, Vol. I, No. 1, 1919.

[129]   *Melbourne A Century of Memories: The Melbourne Centennial Book*, Melbourne Area Chamber of Commerce Centennial Committee, 1980.

[130]   The *Kentucadet*, Vol. XVIII, No. 2, November 1947. The *Listening Post*, Vol I, No. 1, 1919. Miss Faircloth's calling card was found in a scrapbook belonging to Cadet Thomas Kildow, KMI class of 1919.

interesting to know if any of the cadets knew the first Mrs. MacArthur, the former Louise Brooks, who was also a socialite from Palm Beach.

One of the most persistent problems addressed by Colonel Fowler was the perception by many people that military schools were where parents sent sons who were troublemakers or uncontrollable. One section of the KMI catalogs and information booklets published during Fowler's administration was entitled "We Are Not a Reform School":

> So many people have an idea (aided by our would-be competitors) that only bad boys are sent to military schools, that we ask your special attention to the following paragraph.
>
> This section is intended for parents who have really bad boys, and a little plain talk now may save future trouble. There are a great many different kinds of "bad boys" (depending upon the point of view of the observer), for most of whom we have a hearty sympathy, but drinking, gambling, lying, and kindred vices will not be tolerated under any circumstances. We have a set of gentlemen here, and we will not allow any other kind of boy to remain long after he shows he is the "other" kind: and if it appears that he has been expelled from another school, our rates for him will be doubled, and even then the school will probably be the loser, as such boys do not pay at any price.
>
> We are determined to make this school a safe place for the average boy, and not a reputable retreat for the disreputable scions of disappointed parents. When in our judgment a boy is a detriment to the school, we reserve the right to send him home without preferring specific charges.[131]

The retirement of Colonel Fowler from all but ceremonial duties after commencement on May 23, 1919, began a six-year period of serious problems for KMI.

---

[131]   Catalog, 1914-1915, p. 17.

Chapter IV

---✦---

THE TIME OF TROUBLE

Colonel Guy A. McGowan assumed the duties of superintendent upon Colonel Fowler's retirement. McGowan had joined the KMI faculty in 1901, and Colonel Fowler had groomed him to become superintendent upon his retirement. Shortly after assuming the superintendency, McGowan died of a heart attack while visiting his father's farm. Although fondly remembered by the cadets, McGowan had little lasting impact on the school.

On October 19, 1919, Colonel Edmund L. Gruber resigned from the Regular Army to accept the position of superintendent of KMI. The colonel appeared to be an excellent choice as the new superintendent. He had graduated from West Point in 1904, and after being commissioned, he served in numerous assignments with various artillery units. From 1915 to 1917, he had been an instructor in the tactics department at West Point. During World War I, he again served in various artillery units. Prior to resigning his commission in 1919, he was assigned to the War Plans Division of the War Department General Staff. He would only remain as superintendent until May 20, 1920, when he resigned his position to reenter the army. Colonel Gruber's major accomplishment during his short tenure as superintendent was to get the school through the aftermath of a disastrous fire in Eau Gallie.

Two changes made when Colonel Gruber became superintendent were a change in the name of the school paper and the formal establishment of the Honor System. For twenty-three years, the *Cadet Adjutant* had been published quarterly. Some believed that it was the oldest paper published at a military school in the country. The new publication was published biweekly and called the *Listening Post*.

In the first issue of the *Listening Post*, the editors spelled out the purpose of the paper and indicated that the school was changing in some significant ways:

> The Listening Post aims to bring us all closer together; to unite us with a school spirit such as never before has been had by any other school, and to provide a history for K.M.I. that can be understood by all.
>
> A new era has dawned for K.M.I. a more liberal spirit has been introduced, and we all feel that a quarterly paper, published in an indifferent manner and at irregular intervals, is not good enough for the faculty and cadets of this institution. Therefore, we have prepared the first issue of The Listening Post as befits a school of our standing.[132]

The most important of the changes was the establishment of the Honor System, a system that would remain in place until the school closed and would become the basis for the Honor System at Kentucky Country Day. Without giving many details on the actual working of the Honor System, the *Listening Post* urged all of the students to support the implementation of the new system:

> The establishment of the Honor System means that the school officers have confidence in you and me: that it intends to entrust to us the government of our own actions, and it depends upon us to live up to our consciences, nothing more. Certainly this should be easy enough for all. There is not a man in school who has not a conscience and a sense of honor and the only thing else necessary is the inclination to follow the dictates of our own consciences. This sounds quite simple, but it is unfortunate that there was a few men in school who, either deliberately or otherwise, attempt to "get away with it," and take advantage of the new system. These men merely injure

---

[132]   The *Listening Post*, Vol. I, No. 1, Fall, 1919.

themselves and the rest of the school, without gaining any advantage for either themselves or the school thereby.[133]

Although there were few details about the Honor System, it was clear that the cadets were being given more responsibility for their conduct and the conduct of the entire cadet corps. "The establishment of the Honor court makes another step forward in student government. The court was selected from all academic classes, and consists of three seniors, two juniors, one sophomore and one freshman. One of the seniors holds the position of president. It is the duty of the Court to try all cases of violations of the Honor System, and judge such cases absolutely impartially."[134]

Another change was the abolition of the old literary societies, which the editors of the *Listening Post* announced, "Gone are the days of the old Literary Societies, the days when one went to a Society because he had to, and vainly stuttered and strangled trying to pronounce the name of the particular society to which he belonged. The so-called 'Literary Societies' were excellent—as sleep inducers—and they provided considerable amusement for those who were not on the program or asleep."

To replace the old societies, three new clubs were established: the Dramatic Club, the Glee Club, and the Outdoor Club. Membership in the new clubs was not compulsory and each was designed to appeal to the different interests of the cadets. The Dramatic Club was intended to develop the theatrical talents of the cadets and present plays to the battalion. The Glee Club would develop an appreciation of music among its members and provide entertainment for the other cadets. The Outdoor Club would bring its members closer to nature and instruct them in how their forefathers had lived.[135]

Yet another change that was greeted with great enthusiasm by the cadets was a change in the dress uniform. The new uniform was described as having a high-waisted, form-fitting coat with short lapels and natural shoulders. It was blue gray in color and could be worn with gray or white trousers or gray breeches. If the coat was worn with the gray breeches, then spiral puttees of the same color were to be worn. Rank insignia was to be worn on the sleeves and lapels of the new coat. The editors of the

---

[133] Ibid.

[134] Ibid.

[135] The *Listening Post*, Vol. I, No. 1, Fall 1919.

Listening Post were of the opinion that "probably no change that has ever taken place here has met with such unanimous enthusiastic approval as the announcement of the change in uniform equipment. Possibly no greater step forward was ever made. The change was radical, yes, but if it involves a little radicalism to depart from a precedent that never should have been established, then we are justified in that departure."[136]

On January 20, 1920, a fire broke out in the central section of the barracks in Eau Gallie. The last inspection of the barracks had been at 1:00 a.m., but by 3:00 a.m. when the fire was discovered, the barracks was heavily involved, and the fire was completely out

Bayonet Practice in the Sun—Kaufmann

of control. The fire had apparently started in the classroom area on the first floor of the building, an area not inspected at 1:00. Six faculty officers who lived in the central section of the building immediately began alerting the sleeping cadets and started to remove property from the building. All of the cadets managed to evacuate the building safely without any serious injuries. Colonel Gruber attributed the fact that no one was seriously injured to the military training and discipline of the cadets. He was certain that without that discipline, there probably would have been a mob scene and potentially some loss of life.

The entire building was consumed in less than an hour. All of the nearby cottages and the pavilion were saved, in part by the favorable direction of the wind but primarily by the effort of the cadets who fought the fire when it appeared about to spread to the buildings. Colonel Gruber singled out nine cadets for their heroic efforts.

Cadets Donald Webb and Eldo Maple alerted fellow students and helped them

Cleaning Up After the Fire—Beard

---

[136] The *Listening Post*, Vol. I, No. 1, 1919.

remove their personal property from the burning building. In doing so, they both lost all of their own property. Cadet James Saunders devoted his time to protecting Cottage 10 by extinguishing several fires that might have spread to other cottages. He was finally removed from his post, completely exhausted. Cadet William Nailling, working in his bare feet, prevented the fire from spreading to the pavilion. He was also removed from this duty when completely exhausted. Cadet John Curry assisted Nailling in fighting to save the pavilion and continued to work despite the fact that his hands were burned and blistered. Cadet Hugh Steffen carried water to prevent the fire from spreading to the cottages, a task he continued even after falling off the roof of one of the cottages. Cadets John Hightower and Samuel Beare worked tirelessly to save Cottage 9. Cadet Charles Cuthbertson removed the burning awnings from Cottage 10, thereby saving the building and its contents.

As soon as the fire was out, plans were made to issue clothing to those cadets who had lost their personal possessions. Arrangements were also made to house 150 of the displaced cadets in the homes of the residents of Eau Gallie. The school had suffered a significant loss, estimated at $20,000 for the building and nearly $10,000 for school equipment. Insurance would cover a portion of the loss, $13,000 for the building and $2,500 for the equipment. None of the property lost by the cadets was covered by insurance, and there was no estimate of the value of their loss.

The school officials quickly decided that the school would remain in Florida for the rest of the term. Financial considerations played a significant part in the decision. The packing and moving back to Kentucky would have been costly, and it would have taken at least a week to make the necessary arrangements for the movement. In addition, once the cadets were back in Kentucky, they would have to purchase winter uniforms. A plan was quickly devised to move the school into a cantonment, which could be erected quickly. Orders were placed for lumber, tents, cots, mattresses, and mosquito bars. All of the items necessary to construct the cantonment were delivered to the campus in less than three days.

The tents were erected, with wooden floors, in three

Tent City—Beard

company streets each containing twelve sixteen-by-sixteen foot tents. The tents were large enough for eight people, but only five cadets were assigned to each tent. The tents were equipped with electric lights, tables, and chairs. At the end of each company street, washing and toilet facilities were constructed. Living in tents was not a new experience. Cadets had been housed in tents on previous occasions, especially when enrollment exceeded the capacity of the barracks.

Colonel Gruber was of the opinion that many of the cadets would soon prefer living in the tents rather than the old barracks rooms. The weather was warm, and the temperature was expected to continue to increase before the school left Florida. He stated, "When the hot days are really here, everyone will look back upon the fire as a blessing in disguise." If a cadet didn't want to live in a tent, the cottages were still available.

Academic instruction was conducted in eight large tents and study hall was held in the pavilion. The instructors who had lived in the barracks were housed in small four-wall tents erected at the end of each company street. Thus, the school continued to operate almost without interruption until it returned to Kentucky.

Apparently, some of the cadets used the fire as an excuse to withdraw from school. They informed their parents that it would cost nearly $500 to replace the items they had lost in the fire. The school estimated that the largest amount needed would be $200, and this would

The Pavilion—Beard

apply only in a few cases. The school was willing to furnish items to those cadets who had lost them: a complete khaki uniform, consisting of coat, breeches, OD shirt, belt, and a pair of tan shoes, leggings, hat, black tie, and a pair of blankets, mosquito bar, mattress, and cot to be used until the end of the term.

Another financial problem was caused by parents sending money directly to their sons to replace items lost in the fire. The school requested that any future checks be sent to the school and made payable to Kentucky Military Institute. A letter explaining what the money was to be used for should accompany the check. If the parents desired, they could designate an amount for a weekly allowance, the recommended amount was $1.50.

The letter cautioned that "if parents persist in sending unusual sums directly to their boys, they alone are responsible for joy rides, run-away parties, gambling and the resultant punishment when their boys are caught."

Colonel Gruber concluded his long letter with a telling statement: "The plans for the future development and expansion of K.M.I. are now under consideration. Undoubtedly the destruction of our barracks in Florida will have a material influence in determining these plans. As soon as they have been definitely formulated, our patrons will be acquainted with their content."[137]

After spending nearly three months in tents, the cadets boarded the KMI Special to return to Kentucky. The normal rush of events leading up to commencement would occupy most of their time. Following commencement, Colonel Gruber resigned his position as superintendent and returned to the army. Despite his distinguished military career, which ended with Brigadier General Gruber's untimely death on May 30, 1941, he would be remembered primarily for writing "The Caisson Song." As a young lieutenant with an artillery unit in the Philippines, Gruber and several others wrote the first verse, and then he added other verses. On November 11, 1956, Gruber's melody, with new lyrics, was dedicated as "The Army Song."[138]

A new classroom building was completed at Eau Gallie just before the cadets returned in January 1921. The new building, built to replace the classrooms lost in the fire the previous year, consisted of eight classrooms. Each room was well lighted and heated with electric stoves and were furnished with new desks and chairs.[139] There is no information concerning the construction of new barracks to replace the one lost in the fire. The 1921 *Saber* reported that "because of the excellent climatic conditions, most of the cadets have lived in floored tents for the past two years."[140]

---

[137] Information on the Eau Gallie fire is contained in a letter from Col. Gruber, "A Statement to Our Patrons," February 2, 1920, Letter found in the Jack Morgan materials.

[138] http://sill-www.army.mil/FAMAG/1926/Jul_Aug_1926/Jul_Aug_1926_full_edition.pdf.

[139] The *Listening Post*, Vol. II, No. 3, January 1921.

[140] *Saber*, 1921, p. 139.

The trip to Florida was still an adventure for the cadets, but the process was well practiced:

> K.M.I. had made the Florida trip for sixteen successive years, and for this reason the journey is made without any hitches. All packing is done during the Christmas holidays, and the freight cars are loaded on the day previous to our departure. On the day set for leaving Kentucky, a special train of sleeping cars pulls up to the school, and in a few minutes the entire school personnel is entrained and on their way to the Land of Eternal Sunshine.[141]

Although the trip to Eau Gallie had become routine over the years, the life of the cadets was anything but routine. They found the stay in Florida to be both interesting and educational. A few days after their arrival in 1921, the cadets were entertained by the members of the Eau Gallie Yacht Club in their "palatial" clubhouse. The

Cadets Visit Umbrella Rock on Lookout Mountain Tennessee—Kaufmann

social activities continued the entire time the cadets were in Florida. Additionally, many of the cadets had the opportunity to visit the winter resorts of Palm Beach, Daytona, Miami, and St. Augustine.

Despite all of the activities, "these diversions became old. Ocean bathing was all right, but its novelty soon wore off. One boating trip was very much like any other. Palm Beach wasn't much of a place after all. Eau Gallie was a nice town, but why the dickens didn't they have a show once in a while." The lure of the Blue Grass State was calling, and the cadets were ready to go home. However, they anticipated their return the following year and expressed the hope that they would be able to host dances in their newly constructed barracks.

---

[141] Ibid.

The trip home was filled with various stops for sightseeing and meals. The first stop was in St. Augustine for breakfast and tours of the city's historic sites. In the afternoon, the school baseball team played a game against the Duvall High School team from Jacksonville. The next stop was in Jacksonville for supper and more sightseeing. About noon the next day, they stopped in Chattanooga for more tours of the historic sights. Because there were so many things to see, the cadets divided into groups and went their separate ways. Presumably, this allowed those cadets who had been to Chattanooga on previous trips to see places they had not seen before:

> We arrived at Military Park, Kentucky, at seven o'clock Sunday morning. By noon everything was unpacked and in its proper place. In the afternoon many of our friends called on us. In the evening the usual study period was held, and the next morning classes were resumed. Everybody was glad to be back, for after all, Kentucky is God's Country.[142]

In January of 1921, Cadets Smith and Sanford were credited with saving the life of a Mrs. Dongan. The cadets witnessed Mrs. Dongan's car roll off the Eau Gallie River Bridge into the water. The two cadets dove into the river and managed to free the unconscious woman who was trapped under her car. Mrs. Dongan was lifted by means of a rope to the surface of the bridge where she was revived by other cadets. She was taken to the Military Inn, where she eventually recovered from her injuries.[143]

Sheldon Ford followed Colonel Gruber as superintendent. He had joined the KMI faculty as a mathematics teacher in 1907. He had been appointed headmaster when Guy McGowan was advanced to the position of superintendent. Ford was well liked by the students and alumni, and a number of letters were written to the board of visitors urging his selection as superintendent. Colonel Ford immediately set about trying to improve the school's financial position following the fire at Eau Gallie. Perhaps overwhelmed by the numerous financial problems facing the school, Ford left in June of 1921 to pursue a career in higher education.

---

[142] *Saber*, 1921, pp. 139-145.
[143] The *Listening Post*, Vol. II, No. 3, January 1921.

A little stability was given to the school by the return of Major David Byars as the professor of Military Science and Tactics and Commandant in 1920. Byars had graduated from KMI in 1903 and had then taught there for three years before entering West Point in 1906. He graduated from the Military Academy in 1910 and was commissioned in the Regular Army. After serving in a number of different positions, he was assigned as the PMS&T at the University of Kentucky in 1919. The

Major and Mrs. Ford on Left and Colonel and Mrs. Fowler on the Right—Kaufmann

1921 *Saber* noted: "We realize that we are unusually fortunate in having an 'old boy' as commandant. Major Byars was a 'kaydet' just as we are once upon a time. He realizes that we must raise cain occasionally and altho he never hesitates to give us the punishment the Blue Book prescribes, we know that he does not hold an occasional infraction of the rules against us."[144]

An interesting innovation was initiated by Colonel Ford when he became superintendent. He wanted the students to organize an athletic association that would be in charge of all things related to athletics at the school. The colonel appointed a committee consisting of two faculty members and three cadets to organize the association. The committee drafted a constitution and a set of bylaws which were adopted by the students.

The Athletic Association's constitution provided that all athletic matters would be managed by an Athletic Council consisting of three cadets elected by the association

Major Byars—Beard

---

144   *Saber*, 1921, p. 24.

and two faculty members appointed by the superintendent. "The Council will handle all athletic funds, arrange all games, award all letters and monograms and make all rules concerning athletics at K.M.I."

Once the plan was implemented, the school would reduce the fixed charges, and each cadet would pay a six-dollar athletic fee. The payment of the fee would entitle the cadets to free admission to all home games and make them eligible for any varsity team. The money from the fee and receipts from home games would be used to pay for away games, uniforms, and other items, such as letters and sweaters. The coaches of the various teams would still be hired and paid by the school, not the association. It was hoped that since the cadets were financially involved in the school athletic program, more interest and support would be generated among the cadets.[145]

To replace Colonel Ford, the board of visitors selected Clinton Sells to be the new superintendent. Sells appeared to be an excellent choice considering the serious financial problems the school faced. He had been a railroad executive for a number of years and had served in a number of administrative positions during World War I. Despite his obvious management skills, Colonel Sells would encounter a problem that would compound the school's financial problems.

On December 21, 1921, a fire destroyed the barracks in Lyndon and seriously damaged the Ormsby Annex and the Edison Science building. When the students returned from Christmas vacation in January, they immediately boarded the KMI Special for the trip to Eau Gallie. The cadets who were still living in tents in Florida would have an extended stay in Florida. The corps would not return to Kentucky until May.[146]

The cause of the Lyndon fire was never determined. James Stephens, in his history of KMI, relates an interview with a former student who was in school at the time of the fire, in which he stated that the fire was started by an angry cadet. The interviewee said that the cadet was never apprehended or punished for his action and would later graduate. Stephens reported that the accuser was a creditable source with a long and distinguished career of public service. Whether the fire was the result of

---

[145] *Saber*, 1921, p. 103.
[146] "KMI Rises from Ruins of Old," The *Louisville Times*, no date, 1922.

arson or not will always be open to question. Whatever the answer, it was most certainly one of the problems that drove KMI into bankruptcy. [147]

The extended stay in Florida was to allow sufficient time for the construction of two new barracks and repairs to the other damaged buildings. When the cadets returned to Lyndon, they found Ormsby Annex and the Edison Science building restored and repainted. One of the new barracks was finished, and the other would be completed before school opened in the fall. The new barracks were built of stuccoed hollow tile and were semi-fireproofed. The barracks were designed to accommodate 150 cadets. Each building contained about forty rooms, and each floor had toilet facilities. A common shower area was located in the basement of what would become known as A Barracks. The buildings were connected to a new steam heating plant, and a new sewage system was installed.

The firm of Nevin, Wischmeyer, and Morgan had designed the new barracks after studying the construction of barracks at a number of other schools. It is interesting to note that the rooms all opened onto open porches, a feature Colonel Gruber had cited as one reason for the safe evacuation of the barracks during the Eau Gallie fire. It was estimated that the new barracks had cost about $90,000. The new barracks would be home to the cadet corps until KMI ceased to exist in 1971. [148]

The senior class of 1922 had experienced four tumultuous years: the retirement of Colonel Fowler, the unexpected death of Colonel McGowan, the brief administrations of Colonels Ford and Gruber, and the appointment of Colonel Sells as well as the two devastating fires.

A Barracks

Cadet Major Allen Murray Beard expressed his hope for the future of the school in his commencement address:

[147] Stephens, op. cit., p. 163.

[148] "150 Cadets Expected at KMI to Reopen in Fall with Prof. J.H. Richmond on its Staff," newspaper article, no paper, no date.

We have learned to love K.M.I. and have done our utmost to maintain the traditions and standards that were handed down to us by previous classes.

As we are about to leave we see our Alma Mater moving into a new home. We know however that new buildings do not mean a new school. We the members of the Senior Class cannot take the tradition and standards of the old school into the new home, but we charge you our fellow cadets to do so. When we return to K.M.I. in years to come we hope to see still more improvements and a still larger school plant but we know that in spite of all changes in building and equipment K.M.I. will still be the same old school, not physically, but in spirit.[149]

There was yet another problem looming on the horizon. KMI did not make the trip to Florida in 1923. Enrollment began to drop until it reached only sixty cadets. Faced with a huge debt and a declining student body, Sells did not open the school for the fall term in 1924, and KMI went into receivership during the fall.

Undoubtedly, the two fires were what forced KMI into receivership. However, the instability of the superintendent's position could not have helped the situation. The constant turnover at the top must have caused some concern for parents who were considering sending their sons to KMI. The prosperity and stability of the Fowler years was gone, and the fate of the school was in serious doubt.

---

[149] Handwritten copy of speech in the Beard Family Papers in the possession of the author.

Chapter V

---•---

NEW OWNERS, NEW LIFE

Information that the Kentucky Military Institute property was in receivership and could be purchased reached Lewisburg, West Virginia. Charles B. Richmond, commandant of cadets at Greenbrier Military School, made the decision to go to Louisville and inspect the school property and its facilities. Richmond had been at Greenbrier since 1916 and commandant since 1917. He was apparently well liked by the cadets because the *Briar Patch*, the school yearbook for 1923, was dedicated to Major Richmond.[150]

What Richmond found in Lyndon was a ninety-six-acre campus with two newly constructed barracks, a repaired classroom building, a freshly painted and repaired administration building, and a gymnasium. He and two partners, Charles E. Hodgin and Samuel B. Marshall, fellow instructors at Greenbriar, made the decision to purchase the closed school. Before the trio could purchase the school, they needed to obtain some financial backing for the venture. They contacted several local businessmen who agreed to back them in the purchase. As soon as the enrollment reached fifty

Charles B. Richmond—1928
Saber

---

150   http://www.wvgenweb.org/greenbrier/schools/brierpatch.htm.

students, the money was released to the partners. Although Marshall would remain with the school for more than forty years, he sold his interest in the school to Richmond and Hodgin after several years. Colonel Richmond would remain the principal owner until his death in 1968.[151]

Dr. William T. Simpson, Richmond's son-in-law and future president of KMI, stated that the colonel purchased the property at the Jefferson County courthouse door. By the spring of 1925, the three partners owned KMI. An undated newspaper article from 1925 announced that KMI would open in September under a new administration. The article predicted that with the support of the alumni and many of the students from the 1923 to 1924 session who vowed to return, the enrollment would probably exceed 150 cadets. "The Kentucky Military Institute promises this fall to reopen as one of the strongest, best-equipped and best directed preparatory schools in the country . . ."[152] The

Charles E. Hodgin—
1928 *Saber*

records indicate that Colonel Sells also sold the Eau Gallie property to a Harold Bredlow in 1925. However, the transaction was never finalized, and Sells retained the property for several more years.[153]

When KMI reopened, it was a high school, although there were frequently cadets present who had completed four years of high school and were taking courses to prepare them more fully for college careers. Enrollments barely reached the number predicted by the newspaper; there were just 153 students in school at the end of the 1925-1926 school year. The number would jump to 175 for the 1926-1927 year but fell back to 131 in the next year. Colonel Richmond, his new title, started to recruit students as soon as the school was purchased. He dispatched faculty members across Kentucky and the neighboring states looking

---

[151]   William T. Simpson to the author, January 27, 2012; E-mail, William T. Simpson to the author, February 22, 2013.

[152]   "150 Cadets Expected at KMI to reopen in Fall with Prof. J. H. Richmond on Its Staff," Newspaper, no name, no date, 1925, in the author's possession.

[153]   Abstract for Eau Gallie property from the earliest public records of Brevard Co. Fla., to and including the 24th day of May A.D. 1947.

for prospective students. He also worked to get the school much-needed publicity. Recruiting students and gaining favorable publicity for the school would be Colonel Richmond's lifetime work.

On November 23, 1927, four cadet buglers participated in the grand opening of the Temple Theatre in Louisville. Present at the opening were Governor William T. Fields, governor-elect Flem D. Sampson, Mayor Joseph T. O'Neil, and mayor-elect William B. Harrison. The entire corps had been invited to the opening, but because of an early trip the next morning to Ashland for a football game, they were unable to attend. The invitation might have been helped by the fact that the president of the Temple Theatre, J. E. Dunn, was the father of Cadet Charles Dunn.[154]

The next month, the entire cadet battalion participated in the Inaugural Parade for Governor Sampson in Frankfort. The cadets boarded a train at Military Park, as the Lyndon stop directly across LaGrange road from the school entrance was frequently called, at 8:30 a.m. There were three chair cars reserved for the battalion. The *Kentucadet* reported, "Although the cadets were handicapped by having a band in their rear and none in front to march to, they made the best show in the parade, according to many witnesses of authority, also the great amount of applauding as the cadets swung down the avenue was greatly appreciated and it proved to them they were welcome guests in Frankfort."[155]

By the beginning of the 1928-1929 school year, it appeared that the recruiting efforts were beginning to pay dividends. The *Kentucadet* announced that enrollment was the highest in KMI history with over two hundred cadets enrolled. Both barracks, the quarters in Ormsby Hall and Fowler Hall, were all filled to capacity. The paper concluded, "Effective advertising of increased facilities and the stimulation of activity among friends and alumni are held responsible for the development of the Lyndon institution."[156]

In the *Kentucadet* for October 13, 1928, Colonel Richmond welcomed new and returning cadets with words of pride and enthusiasm for the coming year:

---

[154] The *Kentucadet*, Vol. 2, No. 2, December 16, 1927.

[155] The *Kentucadet*, Vol. 2, No. 2, December 16, 1927.

[156] The *Kentucadet*, Vol. XXXIII, No. 1, October 13, 1928.

In this, the first issue of "The Kentuckucadet [sic]." It is my desire to extend a word of greeting to new friends and old, who have assembled in such numbers that we face a new year with the greatest enrollment in the history of the Institution.

Larger numbers mean added responsibilities on the part of the administration, increased equipment for instruction, and new faculty members. These requirements have been met. Better than this phase, however is the fact that our continuous progress in the past has attracted favorable attention and friendly assistance, which has made possible two new buildings—the gymnasium and Fowler Hall.

Our greatest pride, though, transcends these material indications and rests upon our most valuable possession—the long line of distinguished and loyal men who have gone from Kentucky Military Institute to make history for themselves and the nation . . . . [157]

The effort to involve the parents and alumni in the recruitment of new students paid off in other ways. At the 1928 homecoming, a new gymnasium, valued at $35,000 was dedicated. The money to construct the new building had been donated by alumni and patrons of the school. The

The New Gymnasium—1932 Catalog

new facility was built of white brick and concrete, and its architecture was intended to match the other campus buildings. The building was completely equipped for basketball, volleyball, track, and other indoor sports. The basement had shower facilities, dressing rooms, wrestling rooms, and an indoor rifle range.

Also in use for the first time in 1928 was Fowler Hall, a separate school for younger boys. The building was located at the back of the campus, away from the Upper School buildings. The building was steam

---

[157] The *Kentucadet*, Vol. XXXIII, No. 1, October 13, 1928.

heated and had modern plumbing facilities. The Junior School was completely self-contained, with living and school facilities all located in

Fowler Hall. The Junior School consisted of students in the first through eighth grades and was preparatory for advancing to the high school. The cadets in the Junior School had their own daily schedule of activities. Their only real interaction with the high school cadets was at meal time.

Basketball Game in the New Gymnasium—1930 Catalog

The Junior School had its own military organization, and the discipline was similar to the Upper School, but modified because of the age of the students. Living with the cadets was a housemother who was

charged with maintaining a homelike atmosphere. The rooms were swept and the beds made by a janitor. However, the boys were held responsible for the general neatness and cleanliness of their rooms.

Fowler Hall—1930 Catalog

Fowler Hall had its own commandant of cadets who, along with his wife and the other teachers, lived in the building with the cadets. The military training was under the direction of the Fowler Hall commandant. An inspection was held before each meal to make sure that the cadet's hands and faces were clean, their shoes polished, and hair combed. Cadets who demonstrated the necessary ability were made officers and wore distinctive chevrons. Fowler Hall had its own guard detail consisting of an officer of the day, corporal, and bugler.

The cadets in the Junior School also had their own separate playground and drill field. There were a number of athletic teams,

Fowler Hall Football Player—1930 Catalog

including football, basketball, and baseball. The Fowler Hall cadets also had their own special time to use the facilities of the new gymnasium. Each of the young cadets was required to participate in some sort of recreational activity every afternoon.

Although the Fowler Hall cadets ate in the main dining hall, they sat at separate tables with their teachers. Mealtime was a time for conversation and instruction in proper manners. The 1928 Catalog said that good food was served and that most cadets gained ten to fifteen pounds in a year. Parents were asked not to send food to their sons, unless it was fruit. One requirement that was the same for Junior and Upper School cadets was the writing of a Sunday night letter to their parents. The 1928 Catalog listed the cost of attendance for the Fowler

Fowler Hall Cadets and Mail from Home—1930 Catalog

Hall cadets to be the same as for Upper School cadets. By 1932, the cost for attending Fowler Hall was $100 less than for the senior school.

The 1928-1929 Catalog stated, "Experience has taught us that the busy boy is the happy boy, and the Fowler Hall cadets are busy, either at work or at play, from reveille until taps. They lead a systematic and active life. They acquire an erect carriage; learn to be polite and truthful, and to obey promptly and cheerfully. The benefits of such training, both in leadership and in character, remain with them for life."[158]

The Junior School Schedule

6:20	Reveille
6:30	Sitting up exercises
6:50	Personal inspection of cadets
7:00	Breakfast
7:30	Inspection of quarters

---

[158] 1928-1929 KMI Catalog, p. 128.

8:00 to 12:30	Study and recitations

Note—11:00 to 11:10 Recess, boys are served with graham crackers and milk or sandwich

1:00	Lunch
1:30	Assembly and distribution of mail
2:00 to 3:00	Military drill
3:30 to 4:30	Athletics
4:30 to 5:30	Bathing and dressing
5:45	Inspection of person and quarters
6:00	Dinner
7:00 to 7:30	Study for all grades
5-minute recess	
7:35 to 8:15	Study for grades 6th, 7th, and 8th
7:35 to 8:00	Quiet period and storytelling in lounge for small boys
8:00	Taps for small boys
8:30	Taps for 6th, 7th, and 8th grades

The daily schedule for the Upper School cadets in 1928 was as follows. It would remain essentially unchanged and would be familiar, with only a few modifications, to cadets for the rest of the school's history.

6:00 a.m.	Reveille and sitting-up exercises
6:40 a.m.	Police Inspection
7:00 a.m.	Breakfast
7:25 a.m.	Sick Call
7:30 a.m.	Guard Mount
7:45 a.m.	Chapel
8:05 a.m. to 12:55 p.m.	Study and recitations
1:15 p.m.	Luncheon
2:20 to 3:05 p.m.	Drill
3:05 to 5:55 p.m.	Recreation
6:00 p.m. (Monday, 6:30 p.m.)	Retreat, roll call, dinner
6:30 to 7:00 p.m.	Social Period
7:00 to 9:20 p.m.	Night Study
7:00 to 9:00 p.m.	Inspection by faculty
8:50 p.m.	Tattoo—roll call
9:00 p.m.	Call to quarters

9:10 p.m.	Taps—lights out, in bed
9:40 p.m.	Inspection by faculty
11:00 to 12:00 p.m.	Inspection by faculty
2:00 to 3:00 a.m.	Inspection by faculty

Sunday Changes

7:00 a.m.	Reveille and setting-up exercises
8:00 a.m.	Breakfast
8:25 a.m.	Sick call
8:30 a.m.	Guard mount
10:30 a.m.	General Inspection of barracks
1:00 p.m.	Dinner
3:00 p.m.	Chapel
3:45 p.m.	Dress parade and retreat
6:00 p.m.	Supper
7:00 p.m.	Chapel, YMCA
8:00 to 8:50 p.m.	Letter writing to parents

In 1928, the school purchased a number of horses for use by the cadets. The administration believed that there were many benefits to be derived from riding and felt that it would always be popular with the cadets. The riders could use a number of bridle paths near the school as well as the large open areas of the campus. The activity was so popular that in the fall and spring, all of the horses were in use every afternoon from drill until dinner. To accommodate the young cadets of Fowler Hall, several ponies were purchased so that they could learn to ride and enjoy the same benefits as the older cadets. There was a .75 cents an hour fee for the use of the horses.[159]

Parents could make arrangements with the school for their sons to remain at the school for the entire year. It was felt that this would be beneficial for those boys who might be orphaned or homeless. The school also believed that it might appeal to parents who were on extended trips. One of the selling points was that the school's rural location made it an excellent place for a summer vacation.[160]

---

[159] Catalog for Kentucky Military Institute, 1929-1930, p. 59.
[160] Catalog for Kentucky Military Institute, 1929-1930, p. 61.

At some point, Colonel Richmond started the practice of allowing some young men to attend KMI without paying tuition. The only person that is definitely known to fall into this group is James W. Settle, a 1931 graduate who was an orphan and a resident of Ormsby Village. In his biography, *The Beanery, A Village Named Ormsby*, Settle

Out for an Afternoon Ride—Young

recounts his years at KMI in which it appears that he was a day student and returned to Ormsby Village in the evenings. Other students worked at various jobs at the school to help defray the cost of their tuition. Several alumni have told the author that either their tuition or that of their brothers was waived by Richmond when the family had financial problems. How many cadets fell into this group will never be known, but it shows a little known side of Colonels Richmond and Hodgin.[161] Over the years, numerous other cadets held jobs that helped defray the cost of tuition and living expenses. The cadets held a variety of jobs as barbers, staff assistants, waiters, and kitchen assistants. It is fairly certain that a number of the cadets who held these jobs would have been unable to attend KMI without the credit they received from their work.

Another cadet related that he attended KMI on what he called a scholarship. When Chester Travelstead graduated from Bowling Green High School at the age of sixteen, his mother considered him too immature to go to college, so she sought to enroll him at KMI. However, the $900 tuition was more than she could afford, so she negotiated a reduction by half with the school. To earn the reduction, Chester played his trumpet in the marching band and the dance orchestra. Travelstead would eventually become the Dean of the College of Education at the University of South Carolina. In 1955, he gave a speech on the importance of integration at the university. Shortly after the speech, the university's board of trustees notified him that his contract would not be renewed. He was subsequently

---

[161]   James W. Settle, *The Beanery: A Village Named Ormsby*.

offered the position of dean of the college of education at the University of New Mexico, a position he held from 1956 until his retirement in 1968. Although he only attended KMI for a year, he exemplified the meaning of "Character Makes the Man." He was quoted as saying, "Educators must take the lead in what is right and not be afraid to standup for principles that they hold." Nearly fifty years after he attended KMI, Travelstead wrote a series of short pieces on his experiences at the school.[162]

The 1929-1930 Catalog listed the names of five faculty members who would be familiar to KMI cadets through the late 1960s: (1) Colonel Richmond, president and instructor of Latin; (2) Major Hodgin, headmaster and instructor of history; (3) Major Marshall, commandant and instructor of Mathematics; (4) Captain Groseclose, instructor of mathematics and Latin; and (5) Captain John Pace, coach of athletics and instructor of English. Captain Groseclose had been an instructor with the three partners at Greenbriar Military School, and he had planned to come to KMI in 1925, but illness delayed his arrival until 1926. Captain Pace also joined the faculty in 1926 but would leave for ten years during the Great Depression. He returned to KMI in 1941 as a coach and instructor until he left in 1965 to accept a coaching position at Westport High School in Oldham County, Kentucky.[163]

By 1929, drawing upon the long history of the school, most of the rules and regulations had been established. With the exception of some modifications caused by changing times and experience, most of the rules and regulations would apply for the next forty years. The 1929-1930

---

[162]   Travelstead, Chester C., "The Year at the Kentucky Military Institute," http://www.unm.edu/~ddarling/V6.html; "Buttons are for Buttoning," http://www.unm.edu/~ddarling/v6v1s1.html; "Mr. Day, a Band Director not to be Forgotten," http://www.unm.edu/~ddarling/v6v2s1.html; "The President's Errant Brother," http://www.unm.edu/~ddarling/v6v4s1.html; "Join the Marines and See the World," http://www.unm.edu/~ddarling/v6v5s1.html; "I thought you Said We were Invited to Supper," http://www.unm.edu/~ddarling/v6v7s1.html; "Didn't anyone give you the Signal," http://www.unm.edu/~ddarling/v6v6s1.html; "Victor John Mature and Gilmore James Backus," http://www.unm.edu/~ddarling/v6v8s1.html; "No School on Monday," http://www.unm.edu/~ddarling/v6v3s1.html and http://www.ed.sc.edu/museum/travelstead.

[163]   Catalog for Kentucky Military Institute, 1929-1930, pp. 20-25.

Catalog clearly stated the basic purpose of KMI, and that mission would change little over the next forty-one years. The fundamental mission of the school was to prepare its students for college or to take on the responsibilities of life. "With us, education means the symmetrical development of soul, heart, mind, and body, for we believe that Christian character, gentlemanly baring, good scholarship, and a rigorous body are the results to be desired in education. Upon these fundamental principles have the policies of our school been established."[164]

The first educational goal was to build a strong Christian character. The administration of the school believed that the spiritual life of the boys was of the highest importance. The school was completely nondenominational; consequently, all cadets were required to attend a short chapel service held at morning assembly and the longer Sunday chapel service. Much of the character building was based on the proper regard for honor, which was reflected in the Honor System. "Matters of honor comprise: giving or receiving help with written work, going off school bounds without permission, lying, and stealing . . . The system is a live

Machine Gun Training—1930 Catalog

issue. Each student is on his honor to uphold it by conducting himself as a gentleman; also, by reporting violations, whether of himself or of others, to the student council."[165]

The fact that the school was nondenominational was reflected in the Cadet Prayer, which came into use at some point:

Morning Exercise—1930 Catalog

---

[164] Catalog for Kentucky Military Institute, 1929-1930, p. 41.
[165] 1935-1936 Catalog, p. 23.

Eternal God Our Father whose sons we are, give us a high sense of strengthening comradeship upon this our campus. Guide us that we may not be too severely tempted. Give us grace to live our lives together and save us from weak excuses. Incline our hearts to support those who seek to build a better world and instill in us the qualities that shall produce in the days to come an honest, truthful, courageous noble-minded character. Amen.

Concerning discipline, the true meaning of the word was applied:

Properly it means the training of the mind and body to fit the boy for his life's work; to teach him self-control that he may be fit to control others; to teach him the value of time that he may not waste it; and to teach him in countless ways the meaning of the word *duty*. Discipline is secured mainly by cultivating the pupil's self-respect and appealing to his sense of honor . . . . The discipline of the school is strict but not burdensome. Students are expected to comply with all rules in a cheerful and soldierly manner. No excuse, except that of actual illness, is accepted for failure to perform duty.[166]

The school requested that parents not ask for special privileges for their sons. It was pointed out that privileges were earned through the school's merit system. Each day, merits were awarded for such things as good conduct and scholarship. The cadets could use their merits to obtain certain privileges. "Is it not obvious that the extent of a student's privileges depends upon himself." It is interesting to note that the 1932-1933 Catalog makes only one mention of demerits. When a cadet's conduct was unsatisfactory, he would be counseled and encouraged to improve his conduct. Only after these measures had failed would penalties be assessed. Those penalties might be in the form of demerits, extra drill, or confinement to certain boundaries on campus.[167]

---

[166]   Ibid., p. 24.
[167]   Catalog for Kentucky Military Institute, 1932-1933, p.

A cadet's word was to be accepted as the truth. If he was suspected of some violation of school rules, he was expected to answer truthfully. If he was found to be lying in his response, the penalty could be severe. A cadet was expected to report violations of rules and regulations not only by other cadets, but also by himself. The fact that a cadet's word could not be trusted was soon known throughout the corps, and he was treated accordingly. There were only three appropriate answers to a question from someone in authority. More than seventy-five years after Colonel Richmond acquired the school, Gerry Brinker, a terminally ill 1959 graduate, posted a note on the KMI website. He concluded with a statement summing up the concept of honor and discipline instilled in the cadets. On February 15, 2008, he wrote, "Now, the time is near for me to report to my tactical officer, God. No doubt He will question me. As His Cadet, there will be only three valid answers from me: 'Yes Sir!'; 'No Sir!' and 'No excuse, Sir!'"[168]

REGULATIONS

A copy of the regulations covering conduct and discipline (called the Blue Book) is placed in the hand of each cadet upon entrance. New orders are issued as circumstances require. The following regulations are suggestive of all.

Cadets shall be under the authority of the Institute from the time of their arrival until their departure at the end of the year.

All trunks and suitcases must have the full name, initials, and residence of the owner painted or stenciled on one end, so that in case of loss they may be recovered easily.

A cadet damaging or mutilating property must make an immediate cash settlement. All privileges will be forfeited until he has done so.

Upon receipt of uniform, each cadet will be required to send home his civilian clothes.

---

[168] http://www.kmialumni.org/alumni/roster-main.html, at the Class of 1959 page.

Cadet quarters are subject to inspection at all times by faculty officers. The orderly in charge of the room is held responsible for its condition and contents.

The use of intoxicants or having them in possession is absolutely forbidden. A cadet who violates this rule will be dismissed at once.

No cadet shall engage in gambling.

No cadet shall engage in any form of hazing.

No cadet shall use obscene or profane language.

No cadet shall have firearms in his possession.

Every cadet will be required to write a letter home Sunday night, these letters to be gathered at the breakfast formation Monday morning.

A cadet absent from school bounds after call to quarters (9:00 p.m.) without permission is liable to dismissal.[169]

As clearly stated in these regulations, hazing of cadets was strictly forbidden. However, it was noted in the regulations that there were certain restrictions placed upon new students. Under this caveat, the "Rat System," which had operated for years, would continue to operate throughout the school's history. Undoubtedly, excesses crept into the system, but to a large extent it was more of an annoyance to the new cadets. The requirement to shine the shoes and brass of old men, getting up to close windows at five in the morning before the heat was turned on, and other menial chores were simply a part of life to be endured. Besides, if you survived your Rat Year, there would be new Rats the next year to do your bidding.

The Blue Book—Young

The *Blue Book*, first complied by Colonel Fowler, was issued to each new cadet upon his arrival and set forth many of the regulations for the

---

[169] Catalog for 1935-1936, p. 18.

cadets. Unfortunately, the books are undated, so it is extremely difficult to determine exactly when various editions were issued. A careful reading of a number of Blue Books reveals that few changes were made over the years.

While the thirty-plus pages covered a significant number of rules and regulations, there was a regulation that filled in any omissions: "All disorders, neglects, or misbehavior of which cadets may be guilty, though not specifically mentioned in these regulations, are to be punished according to the nature and degree of the offense." Regulation Number 76 was intended to make certain that cadets knew the rules and regulations: "Ignorance of regulations and orders will not be accepted as an excuse for misconduct."[170]

In 1929, cadets who were sixteen years old could smoke a pipe, provided they had written permission from their parent or guardian. They were required to sign a pledge that they would not smoke cigarettes. The rules stated, "Cigarettes are absolutely forbidden." The penalty for smoking cigarettes was almost as severe as the one for drinking. For a first and second offense, he would receive a severe punishment; for a third, he would be expelled.

On September 18, 1928, Victor John Mature and James Gilmore Backus joined the cadet corps. Although neither would graduate, Mature stayed one year and Backus two years. They would become two of the most famous KMI alumni.

According to his application, Mature was fifteen years old and stood five feet nine inches tall and weighed 171 pounds. His application indicated that he was interested in athletics but had no interest in music. Surprisingly, the question asking if he was interested in dramatics was left blank. Victor was to receive a weekly allowance of a dollar and a half.[171] Although his application listed Latin as his favorite subject, he apparently was not an outstanding student. In a note to Colonel Richmond, Mr. Mature said, "Victor [sic] report is not so good any help that I can give you or his instructor I will be glad to be on hand at once. Do not hesitate to be very strict."[172]

---

[170] Undated Blue Book, Regulation 169, p. 34; and Regulation 76, p. 16.

[171] Victor John Mature, Application for Admission to Kentucky Military Institute, September 10, 1928.

[172] M. G. Mature to Colonel Richmond, October 29, 1928.

Mr. and Mrs. Mature were apparently satisfied with Victor's progress at KMI. On April 10, 1929, Colonel Richmond wrote to thank the Matures for reenrolling Victor for the next school year. In less than two weeks, Victor would run afoul of the rules about unauthorized leave.[173] On April 24, Major Samuel Marshall, commandant, wrote to Mr. Mature: "On Monday night your son Vincent left the school grounds after taps and went to Lyndon. He claims that he went to Lyndon in order to get something to eat. He returned to School on the twelve o'clock car." Major Marshall concluded his letter with the comment that he could not understand why the boys had gone AWOL, knowing they would receive one hundred penalty tours and eight weeks confinement to campus. Major Marshall concluded his letter with what might have been a mild understatement: "However, boys will do some very peculiar things."[174]

On July 10, 1929, Colonel Richmond wrote Mr. Mature, requesting that his account be settled before the new school year began. The colonel stressed that "we are making considerable improvements at KMI this summer and are hard pressed for funds." Across the bottom of the letter is a handwritten note from Mr. Mature saying that Victor was working and would not be returning to school.[175]

Victor Mature—Kaufmann

One persistent story about Mature was that he was expelled from KMI for riding a horse through the dining room. Retired Colonel Park A. Shaw, KMI Class of 1942, recounts that when he met Mature in the 1960s, Victor admitted to the horse riding incident. There were horses at KMI that a high-spirited cadet might have ridden through the mess hall. Perhaps Major Marshall simply neglected to notify Mr. Mature of his son's stunt.[176] Whether the incident actually happened, it became a story passed on by generations of cadets.

---

[173] Colonel Richmond to M. G. Mature, April 10, 1929.
[174] S. B. Marshall to M. G. Mature, April 24. 1929.
[175] Colonel Richmond to M. G. Mature, July 10, 1929.
[176] Park A. Shaw to the author, January 22, 2013.

After leaving KMI, Mature worked at various jobs in Louisville before moving to California to study acting at the Pasadena Community Playhouse. Before getting his first movie contract, a small role in *The Housekeeper's Daughter*, he lived in a tent on a vacant lot for three years. During World War II, he enlisted in the coast guard and made a series of War Bond tours and acted in morale shows. During his movie career, he appeared in more than sixty movies. He died in 1999 at his California home and was buried in the family plot in Louisville.

Much less is known about the career of Jim Backus at KMI. He related that he and Victor Mature both attended KMI "reluctantly." He described the school as "a very fine disciplinary institute of learning."[177] It is interesting that his biography on Wikipedia relates that Backus was expelled from KMI for riding a horse through the mess hall. Backus would go on to appear in over seventy movies, most notably as James Dean's father in *Rebel Without a Cause*. However, he gained his greatest fame as the voice of Mr. Magoo, the cartoon character, and as Thurston Howell III on the television show *Gilligan's Island*.[178]

One frequently overlooked aspect of an education at KMI during the 1930s was the fact that it was possible to take a comprehensive course in commerce and business administration. The course was open only to juniors and seniors who had completed two years of the classical or scientific courses. The course was specifically intended for cadets who had no plans to attend college upon graduation. It was designed to prepare the students to enter the business world immediately upon graduation. The classes were taught by experienced business college teachers and business men. The students were immersed in all of the studies normally associated with the leading business colleges. The two-year course was comprehensive and covered a wide range of subjects from business administration and commercial law to spelling and penmanship. Colonel Richmond admitted that not every boy should go to c[...] helpless Bachelors-of-Arts, as it is[...]

In 1931, the Kentucky Mi[...] formerly the Young Men's Christian Association, took

Cadet Officers—Young

---

177 Jim Backus, *Rocks on the Roof*, p. 84.
178 http://wikipedia.org/wiki/Jim_Backus.

note of a series of articles in the Louisville *Courier-Journal* that illustrated the plight of the poor in the city. At the first meeting of the year, the cadets voted to get the names of two families in the city that needed assistance. At their Sunday night meetings, a collection was taken for the families. Each Tuesday, a committee purchased groceries and delivered them to the two families. The YMCA had been an active organization at the school for a number of years, but this is the only example found of them extending their activities beyond the schools boundaries.[179]

---

[179] *Saber*, 1932.

Chapter VI

---·•·---

BACK TO FLORIDA

O n January 5, 1933, KMI resumed its annual trip to Florida when 175 students along with more than 50 faculty and staff members arrived in Venice. Colonels Richmond and Hodgin had been considering the idea of taking the school to Florida for some time. They had surveyed a number of possible sites on the Gulf Coast to include the Tampa Hotel and several buildings in St. Petersburg. However, the advantages offered by the situation in Venice won them over.

The history of Venice can be traced back to the 1870s, but it would not be until the mid-1920s that its development began in earnest. In 1925, Dr. Fred H. Albee, who had previously developed Nokomis, purchased 2,916 acres of land from the Venice-Sarasota Company. Dr. Albee, an eminent orthopedic surgeon who pioneered work in bone grafting, was convinced of the health benefits of the Gulf Coast. Dr. Albee hired the noted city planner John Nolen to design a town that would be known as Venice. The plan was never implemented because Dr. Albee was approached by the Brotherhood of Locomotive Engineers (BLE) with an offer to purchase his land in 1925, which he accepted. Dr. Albee remained active in the affairs of Venice. In 1933, he purchased the Park View Hotel and established the Florida Medical Center as a very successful teaching hospital.

The BLE was seeking ways to invest the considerable funds it had amassed. In order to do this, the BLE Realty Corporation was established to develop the Venice area, and Nolen was retained to develop a plan for the new city the brotherhood envisioned. The plan that Nolen developed for the BLE was substantially different than the plan he had developed for Dr. Albee. The BLE planned to build a perfect community within three years. They planned to make Venice "The Queen of the Gulf." Venice was to become a retirement community where individuals could either buy farms or homes. Implementation of the plan required the expenditure of huge sums of money. By June 1926, the BLE Realty Corporation was spending an estimated $500,000 a month on the development.

Construction continued throughout the area and "By January 1927, 128,065 feet of sidewalks, 14,195 feet of storm-water pipes, 83,563 cubic feet of paving, 5 miles of electric lines, and 2 miles of street lights and 21 miles of drainage ditches were completed. Streets in Venezia

The Venice Campus—Venice

Park, Gulf View and Edgewood subdivisions were paved, totaling 17.9 miles. On those streets, 191 buildings, totaling $3,160,000 were complete." On May 9, 1927, the state legislature changed the designation of Venice from "town" to "city." The BLE effort seemed well on its way to being a tremendous success.[180]

However, at the BLE convention held in 1927, it was revealed that the BLE Realty Corporation had losses approaching $3.4 million. The four top officers of the brotherhood were removed, and the convention voted to get out of Venice as quickly as possible. By 1928, most of the BLE people had left, and all were gone by 1929. The Brotherhood of Locomotive Engineers had lost $18,000,000 on its investment in "The Queen of the Gulf."[181]

Two of the major structures constructed under the new plan

The Venice Hotel—Young

---

[180] http://www.venicegov.com/archiveslinks/earlyhistory.htm.

[181] "Dreamers of the Past: The Brotherhood of Locomotive Engineers in Venice, 1925-1928," http://scg.co.sarasota.fl.us/Historical resources/Dreamers/ dreamer_ble.asp.

were the Venice Hotel and the San Marco Hotel. The Venice Hotel opened on June 21, 1926; it had one hundred rooms with private baths, a large dining room, and a large ornate lobby. In October 1926, it was announced that the San Marco Hotel would be constructed. The new hotel would have three stories and ninety-two rooms. The San Marco was constructed in only ninety days using concrete block walls and steel columns. It was the most substantial building in Venice and would occasionally be used as a hurricane shelter. Its sturdy construction is probably what eventually saved it from the wrecking ball; it would have cost far more to tear it down than remodel the structure. One interesting feature of the construction was the space between the walls. The cadets discovered that by removing the medicine cabinets in the bathrooms, the smaller cadets could gain entrance into the space. Once inside the walls, the individual could move between the floors and other rooms. The crawl space also allowed access to the roof of the building. A number of the colored tiles on the roof have the names of the adventurous cadets scratched into them as a permanent reminder that they were there.

Despite the rapid beginning, the Great Depression hit Venice and BLE extremely hard. In the early 1930s, the BLE real estate operations went into receivership, and eventually, their holdings were liquidated. During the same period, Venice City employees were not paid, and even the electric street lights were extinguished because the electric bill could not be paid. The city of Venice was virtually deserted; the population was probably less than one thousand. Buildings and houses stood empty, and those few residents who remained eked out a living by fishing and raising vegetables. Alex Hodgin said that his father, Colonel C. E. Hodgin, said that when KMI arrived, "you could see rattlesnakes sunning themselves in the street. That's how much traffic there was."

It was not surprising that the inhabitants of Venice greeted the news that KMI was coming to town with great anticipation. Initially, Colonel Richmond signed a seven-year lease on the two hotels, which had been vacant for several years. Also included in the original lease was a bathhouse located on the gulf, which contained dressing rooms and a shower bath. It took about three months to prepare the buildings for the arrival of the cadets and faculty. The Venice Hotel would house the administrative offices, the faculty, and their families as well as the kitchen and the dining room. The San Marco Hotel would have classrooms and offices on the ground floor and cadet rooms on the upper two floors. The cadet rooms had twin beds with box springs, a tiled bathroom, and other furnishing. The Junior School barracks and the infirmary were located in a smaller building between the Venice and the San Marco. The large open area in front of the San Marco, between Tampa and Venice Avenues, was ideal for a drill area and sports fields. One report stated that the original cost to construct the buildings was $1,000,000. The Orange Blossom Garage was purchased several years later and converted into a gymnasium and offices for the Military Department. It was estimated by one source that the arrival of KMI meant the addition of nearly four hundred jobs to the Venice economy.[182]

The economic impact of the arrival of KMI was almost immediate. The cadets and faculty had money to spend on necessities and entertainment. Parents came to visit their sons and, in some cases, purchased property. The Sunday dress parades held every other week soon began to draw tourists to Venice. In addition, the school held concerts and dances which also brought people to town. Perhaps more importantly, the purchase of fresh fruits, vegetables, and fish to feed the cadets stimulated the local economy. One former mayor of Venice was quoted as saying, "We love the boys, and we also love the money the school brings to town."[183]

Just as the first trip to Eau Gallie had been a time of excitement for the cadets, the first train trip to Venice would have been an adventure. The train left Kentucky and made its way south to the old depot in Venice. The cadets were greeted by a large crowd of well-wishers in Venice. Any problems encountered during

Snow in Lyndon—Brinker

the move have long since been lost in time. The cadets immediately became involved in the affairs of Venice. They arrived on January 4, 1933.

---

[182] http://www.Veniceflorida.com/history.htm. and http://www.gulfcoastliving online.com/KMI.htlm.

[183] "This School Comes South for Winter: When Cold Winds Blow, KMI students, faculty depart for Suncoast Campus," *St. Petersburg Times*, February 12, 1955.

On the seventh, the town held a large reception to welcome the school to Venice and the first Sunday parade was on the fourteenth. Like the move to Eau Gallie, the move to and from Venice would become routine over the years.

When KMI resumed going to Florida for the winter, it joined Riverside Military Academy as the only military schools with two campuses. Riverside, chartered in 1906 in Gainesville, Georgia, began the practice of going to Hollywood, Florida in 1931. The school purchased the Hollywood Hills Hotel and, except for a few years during World War II when the navy used the facilities, the school used the facilities until 1984. The Florida property was sold because of the commercial development around the campus. The funds gained from the sale were used for renovations of the Georgia campus.[184]

The Boys Are Back—Venice

The arrival of the KMI Special was always greeted by the citizens of Venice, especially by many of the town's young ladies. Those cadets who could secure rides to the campus were lucky; those who could not made the walk from the depot to the San Marco. Once at the San Marco, they received their room assignment, unpacked, and then tried to study. The next morning, classes resumed. It was always one of the points driven home about the move to and from Florida; no class time was lost. The travel time was taken from the Christmas break and the spring break, not from school time. Unlike the arrival at Eau Gallie, the cadets did not have to unload the train. Most of the school's equipment and cadets' baggage that would be needed in Florida had been shipped earlier.

In all of the years that the school went to and from Florida, the move was always made by train, except in the spring of 1955. A strike by the non-operating brotherhoods of the railroad made the use of the L&N impossible, and the move back to Kentucky was made by chartered buses.

---

[184] http://www.riversidemilitary.com.

The trip was made in the same time as the train trip. Stops were made along the way for meals and rest stops. The luggage and school equipment was shipped by trucks and vans.[185]

Just as Colonel Fowler had found with the move to Eau Gallie, the health of the students improved, and the number of students on the honor roll increased during the stay in Venice. The fact that the school went to Florida for three months during the winter was also an excellent recruiting tool. The benefits for the health of the students were spelled out in the 1935-1936 Catalog.

Moving from the Depot to the San Marco—Venice

"We escape that problem by going to Southern Florida, the land of sunshine. Here our boys during the recreational period swim in the Gulf, play on the beach, fish, play golf, tennis, baseball, while other schoolboys up north are shivering in icy weather and running the risks of bronchitis, influenza and pneumonia."[186]

One interesting claim for the benefits gained by the Florida session was "Moral and social conditions are likewise improved. All parents know that the danger signal for a boy's morals is set in the winter season, when he is housed up without sufficient outdoor

Cadets Race for the Gulf—Venice

exercise, pure, fresh air, and sunshine. All these causes are removed by spending the winter in Florida, properly supervised, where the greater part of the time is spent in the open." This view of the moral benefit of

---

185 "The KMI Story," The *L&N Magazine*, February 1971.
186 Catalog for Kentucky Military Institute, 1935-1936, p. 86.

spending the winter months in Florida echoed the opinion expressed by Colonel Fowler more than twenty years earlier.[187]

In 1935, Colonel Richmond suggested to Monsignor Charles Elslander of St. Martha's Parish, Sarasota, that a mission be established in Venice. The colonel pointed out that the Catholic students and faculty had to make the trip to Sarasota each Sunday to attend Mass. Initially, Mass was only said during the winter months, when KMI came to town. Mass was held at first in the old Gulf Theater where the altar was set up between the popcorn stand and the soft drink dispenser. Some of the members of the parish remembered sweeping up popcorn boxes and candy wrappers in order to have a place to set up the altar. The first Mass was attended by about twenty people, mostly cadets and faculty members. Eventually, they would be joined by personnel from the Venice Army Air Base and local Catholics.[188]

Over the years, KMI would have a continuing relationship with the Catholic Church in Venice. Following World War II, a campaign was started in Venice to obtain the chapel from the Venice Army Air Base for use as a permanent Catholic Church. Construction on the Venice Army Air Base began in June of 1942, and the base opened the following year. With the conclusion of World War II, the base was closed in 1945, and the property was deeded to the City of Venice in 1947. In anticipation of the transfer of the property to Venice, a campaign was started to obtain the base chapel for use as a Catholic Church. The *Kayemeye Anvil* of March 17, 1946, requested that KMI students, alumni, and parents write letters in support of the efforts to obtain the chapel building. The campaign was successful, and the building was moved to the corner of Tampa Avenue and Nassau Street, a site donated to the Church by Dr. Albee and his wife. Renamed and dedicated in 1947 as the Epiphany Church, the building remained in use until 1980.[189]

Again in 1959, KMI became involved with the Catholic Church when the first Catholic school was opened in Venice. The new school, which was constructed in six months, was not ready when classes were scheduled

[187] Catalog for Kentucky Military Institute, 1935-1936, p. 90.
[188] http://www.epiphanycathedral.org/history.htm.
[189] *Kayemeye Anvil*, March 17, 1946.

to start in the fall. The first students, sixty-six in grades 1-4, attended classes in the San Marco until the new building was completed.[190]

In a series of letters written during the 1930s, Colonel Richmond appealed to the parents of prospective students. In one letter, he explained why KMI was such a bargain. In many respects, the letter, entitled "Speaking of Bargains," was reminiscent of statements made by Colonel Fowler concerning KMI's low tuition twenty years earlier:

Catholic Students Use the San Marco— Epiphany Church

> A great many people, including our competitors, have asked repeatedly how the Kentucky Military Institute finds it possible to give so much school value in a year for so comparatively little money.
>
> They wonder how we can afford to move an entire school to Florida in January. Maintain it there in sumptuous Winter Quarters, bring it back home to Kentucky in April, and still not charge any more tuition than other schools—hardly half as much as some preparatories with equal advantages.

Although the letter addressed the overall cost of tuition at KMI, it focused on how the school could go to Florida and still keep the cost low. The most important factor was that the physical plant had been vacant for several years, and they were rented for a long period at a very nominal rate. It was not overly expensive to move the entire school to Florida. The entire school moved on a special train, consequently the railroad charged the school a low rate for the move. While in Florida, a large sum was saved on the winter fuel bill at the Kentucky location. In addition, the savings on the cost of fresh fruits and vegetables was considerable. The letter concluded, "All in all, it costs us not a great deal more per student to spend

---

[190] http://www.epiphanycathedral.org/history.htm.

our winters in the health giving climate of Florida than it would be to stay in Kentucky . . ." At the time the letter was written, tuition was $950.[191]

Another letter, entitled "We go to Florida to study, to work, and build health!" Colonel Richmond justified KMI's three months in Florida. Apparently, there was some criticism of the move as nothing more than a fun-filled vacation. "Naturally our competitors, having no such Florida winter school advantages, encourage this impression in the minds of parents who are thinking of sending their sons away to school. For business reasons they are obliged to argue that going to Florida involves too many outside distractions that interfere with scholastic duties—lots of play and very little serious work!"

Colonel Richmond argued that if fresh air and exercise were good for growing boys when the weather permitted, how could the weather in Florida not be beneficial? The years of going to Florida had clearly demonstrated that the health of the cadets improved as did the quality of their course work. Colonel Richmond believed that the decision to return to Florida was a complete and unqualified success.[192]

Cadets on the Patio of the Venice Hotel—Venice

Another recruitment letter written during the Great Depression opened with the question "Does your local public school situation present a personal problem for you?" The colonel pointed out that because of current economic conditions, many public schools had been forced to shorten the school year, reduce the number of their teachers, and struggle with overcrowded conditions. All of these factors greatly diminished the

---

[191] Colonel C. B. Richmond, "Speaking of Bargains,'" undated letter.

[192] Colonel C. B. Richmond, "We go to Florida to study, to work, and build health!" undated letter.

ability of the public schools to adequately prepare their students for the demands that the future would force on them.

He was quick to point out that "during this depression the Kentucky Military Institute has steadily added to its faculty, enlarged its course of study, made substantial improvements in the equipment and facilities of both its Kentucky and Florida schools, and—what is most important—has increased the distinctive and vital service of the school, namely, the amount of individual attention and supervision we give to the individual boy." Colonel Richmond concluded, "K.M.I. is in a better position than ever before to help you solve the problem of your son's education. May we not confer with you further about it?"[193]

By the mid-1930s, all cadets were members of one literary society which was divided into various groups. Participation in the society was required of all cadets. The societies met weekly and "the boy learns to think on his feet, to speak with ease in public, to argue and reason, and to appreciate the best in literature." As had been the case with the old societies, much time was devoted to debating.[194]

On April 2, 1936, the *Sarasota Herald* published a long article on KMI and the revival of Venice. The paper gave Colonel Richmond and his decision to bring the school to Venice full credit for beginning the economic revival. Dr. Albee's establishment of the Florida Medical Center and its growing reputation was bringing patients and their families from all around the country. In addition, Dr. Randolph Fried, founder of Bailey Hall, a school for mentally challenged boys in Katonab, New York, founded a school on Treasure Island on land which he leased from Dr. Albee. The article concluded, "The Heads of all these institutions are sold on the idea of Venice as a health center. Their investments and their actions prove that. Parents of KMI students, relatives of patients of the medical center

Cadet Orchestra—Venice

---

[193] Colonel C B. Richmond, "Does your local public school situation present a personal problem for you?" undated letter.

[194] Catalog for Kentucky Military Institute, 1935-1936, p. 64.

and parents of Bailey Hall students all agree that this climate is ideal for the purposes of the institution—and the growing patronage shows that the word is spreading."[195]

One policy which was established by the mid-1930s was the one concerning dances held by the school. The school sent written invitations to the dates of cadets after approving the date. An extract from the dance regulation indicates the rather strict rules governing the conduct of the cadets and their dates:

> Young ladies who attend dances at the Institute shall be accompanied by chaperons to the parlors in Ormsby Hall. There they will be met by the cadets. From Ormsby Hall they shall go direct to the recreation hall, where they shall remain the entire evening. In no case shall either young ladies or cadets be permitted during the dance to leave the building. At the close of the dance, the cadets and young ladies shall go directly to the parlors of Ormsby hall where the latter will be joined by their chaperons. In no case will a cadet be allowed to escort a young lady to or from a dance.[196]

Under no circumstances would permission be given for a cadet to attend dances at other locations.

The rules would be amended in later years to allow the cadets and their dates to leave the gymnasium and walk to Ormsby Hall or the dugout. They were also allowed to walk their dates around the circle in front of Ormsby Hall. At no time during the dance was a cadet to be in an automobile. Any cadet violating the rules was subject to demerits and would not be allowed to attend other dances during the school year. The offending cadet would be confined to his room for four consecutive Sundays, from Vespers until dinner formation. The cadet's date was also punished by not being allowed to attend any dances for the rest of the year. In addition, she would not be allowed to have dates on campus following Vespers Services for the remainder of the year.[197]

---

[195]   *Sarasota Herald*, April 2, 1936.
[196]   Blue Book, Regulation 44, p. 8.
[197]   Blue Book, Regulation 44, p. 11.

As a part of the 1936 homecoming activities, a new dormitory was dedicated to Major Lewis Gregg. Major Gregg was the son of a KMI graduate and the father of a graduate. Before coming to KMI, he had been superintendent of schools for Shelby County for five years and an instructor of mathematics at Georgia Military Academy for two years before arriving in Lyndon in 1920. Major Gregg became ill in 1936 and was unable to teach that year. After surgery, he was able to teach occasionally until 1941. His disease crippled him, and he would be bedridden until his death at the age of ninety-five in 1960. During the last twenty years of his life, he stayed in contact with many of his former

Formal Dance—Venice

students. Major Gregg stated what should be in the mind of a cadet who wanted to be successful: "A thirst for more knowledge; a love of truth; and a desire for a higher life."[198]

In the 1936 Catalog, Colonel Richmond stated the principals upon which KMI would operate until it closed. "It is in a Military School like this that a boy learns daily the lessons of community spirit of personal obligation and responsibility, of co-operation and loyalty, all of which are the fundamental

Gregg Hall—Young

qualities of the good citizen. It is our aim to give a boy an education in keeping with the times, to prepare him for the duties he will encounter when he becomes a man and has a voice in determining the affairs of the nation."[199]

---

[198]   The *Kentucadet*, Vol. XXXV, No. 2, May 1960.
[199]   Catalog for Kentucky Military Institute, 1935-1936, p. 7.

Colonel Richmond was so pleased with the results of the move to Venice that he purchased the property on December 15, 1939. The Venice Archives lists the property owned by KMI: the Venice Hotel, Annex and furnishings; the San Marco Hotel and furnishings—$62,500.00; Orange Blossom Garage—$3,500, purchased in 1939. Between 1943 and 1948, KMI purchased an additional twenty-seven vacant lots for $9,331.17 and one lot with a small residence for $5,500. It is interesting that an article in the *St. Petersburg Times* dated February 13, 1955, states that Colonel Richmond purchased four buildings for $80,000 on a fifteen-year term with no interest.[200]

The Japanese attack on Pearl Harbor on December 7, 1941, came as a shock to the KMI cadets, just as it did to the rest of the citizens of the United States. Although many of the faculty members and cadets had been following the progress of the war around the world, they had no way to anticipate the attack on the United States. Colonel Richmond assembled the cadets in the gymnasium and gave them all the news that he could about the attack and the implications for the country and especially the cadets. The cadets were well aware of the fact that the United States would soon enter the war that was raging in Europe and Asia and that many of them would be called upon to serve their country. President Franklin Roosevelt had signed the Selective Service and Training Act in 1940. That act had established the Selective Service System and required all men between the ages of twenty-one and forty-five to register for the draft. After Pearl Harbor, the act was amended on December 19, 1941, to require all men between the ages of eighteen and sixty-four to register with the Selective Service System. The term of service for those drafted was to be the duration of the war plus six months. It is interesting to note that the director of the Selective Service System appointed in July of 1941, Louis B. Hershey, would be a familiar name to draft age cadets until two years before the school closed in 1971.[201]

Those cadets most immediately affected by the entrance of the United States into the war were the seniors, but all cadets realized that if it were a long conflict, they might all see military service. One member of the senior

---

[200] *St. Petersburg Times*, February 13, 1955.
[201] George Q. Flynn, *The Draft*, 1940-1973, Lawrence, Kansas, University Press of Kansas, 1993, and George Q. Flynn, Louis B. Hershey, *Mr. Selective Service*, Chapel Hill, University of North Carolina Press, 2011.

class who faced the prospect of military service was Park A. Shaw. Although a member of the senior class, he was two credits short of graduation and attended summer school in June and July so that he could enter the army. Before leaving KMI Cadet Shaw and Nancy Watson, the future Mrs. Shaw, would attend the commencement dance, the fourth they attended together, at which Stan Kenton's orchestra played. Shaw would enter the army, go through basic training, and then to Officer's Candidate School at Fort Benning. While at Fort Benning, he discovered that Nelson Hodgin, the brother of Colonel C. E. Hodgin, who had been an instructor at KMI, was also attending OCS. Shaw would eventually be presented his diploma in 1964, which reads "Awarded as of May 1943," by Colonel Richmond and Lieutenant Colonel Hodgin. Also present at the presentation was Park A. Shaw III, Class of 1965.[202]

Another former cadet, Bernard Dahlem, who entered KMI as a twelve-year-old in January of 1942 and graduated in 1946, remembered that eight of the graduates in May of 1942 went straight into the service upon graduation. He relates that it was a very somber time since all of the graduates were sure that they eventually would enter the service. He related that many of the rules and regulations were relaxed during the war years. He remembers that the Cadet Major Al Alfs was the first cadet major to walk the beat. Because there were not enough seniors to fill the possible vacancies, several officers got free passes. They were not busted and kept their

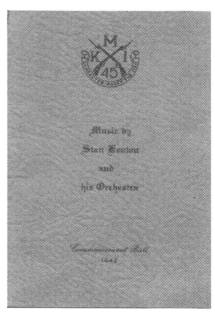

1942 Commencement Dance Card—Young

commissions. Dahlem relates that the cadets were very much aware of the war and that they always received the news of those cadets who had been

---

202 E-mails from A. P. Shaw to the author, January 29, 2013, January 30, 2013, January 31, 2013, and March 26, 2013.

killed. "It seems as though two months didn't go by before we heard that another guy who was right here with us last year was killed! That was a tough way to grow up. I can call up the faces of a dozen or so guys who didn't come back."[203] Dahlem reported that the cadets paid close attention to the progress of the war, knowing where the lines were in Europe and which island would be next in the Pacific. The cadets were well aware that they would soon be in the war.

Although the cadets followed the events of the war, there was little or no change in the academic climate at the school. In one instance, a Captain Chase joined the professor of Military Science and Tactics office and introduced some new training to the school based on changes made during the war. Unfortunately, it will never be known how many former cadets saw service during World War II. After extensive research, James Stephens lists the names of seventy-six former cadets who died during the war, either killed in action or from other causes. Undoubtedly, hundreds of former cadets, whether graduates or not, served in the various branches of the military. Like all of the wars of the United States, there are no good numbers for how many cadets served their country.

The school year that began following World War II saw 295 cadets enrolled. Among this number were 120 New Boys who were welcomed by Colonel Richmond at a special assembly on Tuesday, September 18, 1945. The next three days were taken up by a series of IQ, aptitude, and placement tests. Additionally, the new cadets were issued uniforms, textbooks, rat rules, and name tags. The first drill session was held on Wednesday afternoon and the "old men" returned on Thursday. Short classes were held on Friday for the purpose of making assignments, and normal classes were held on Monday.

A Sunday Parade—McDonald

---

[203] E-mail from Bernard Dahlem to the author, January 31, 2013.

Bernard Dahlem's recollection that some standards were relaxed during the war was addressed by the editors of the *Kayemeye Anvil*, and it appears that the old rules were back in force:

> Yes, students, This War Was Soft—for you! Not for a lot of people. It was hard for you to see your father take his post, you go, and your friend. But, you, in school had to suffer few definite changes or hardships. A democracy knows the value of education, and "School as usual"—taught on!
>
> Now, it's over. Schools are trying slowly to get back to normal. The old concessions that were made in war—speeding up the program, allowing excess credits, and even "coddling" a little in some cases—all there are gone. Schools are hanging up the old sign "Back to usual Pre-War Standards." If you ever let down a little in the past few years, get going now. AND THE GOING IS GOING TO BE TOUGHER!![204]

One of the first changes was the reopening of the golf course which had been closed since 1942. The course had been slightly redesigned. Holes number 7 and 8 were relocated in order not to interfere with the track, and number 9 had been moved so that the lake would not be filled with golf balls. The course had been heavily used since the cadets returned to school. One thing that was normal and would remain a fixture for years to come were the dance classes conducted by Mrs. Francis Crutcher, who had started her classes in 1942. Sixty-seven cadets were enrolled in the classes to be held once a week until Christmas vacation. The classes would resume after the return from Florida in the spring. Mrs. Crutcher was already well known for her annual "End of the Season" dances. Mrs. Crutcher's classes were always popular with the cadets because of the numerous young ladies that came to campus to help with the lessons.[205]

The cadets participated in several activities that brought renewed attention to the corps. On November 11, they marched in the Armistice Day Parade in downtown Louisville. The KMI assembly point was at Fifth and Zane. The parade route was east on Kentucky to Fourth Street

---

[204] The *Kayemeye Anvil*, Vol. 2, No. 2, p. 2.
[205] The *Kayemeye Anvil*, October 14, 1945, p. 3.

and then on Fourth Street to the Ohio River. The cadets, in full dress uniform and with their rifles, were taken to Louisville aboard buses. There was a demonstration at the KMI football game with St. Xavier by what was called a "Trick Drill Unit." The cadets performed such maneuvers as successive to the rear march, present arms, and interchange march. The 1945 performance was the second year that the unit had performed at the ballgame. The Trick Drill Unit was composed of a group of cadets who had volunteered to participate in the demonstration.

After the return to Venice in January 1946, those students who had made the honor roll were permitted to attend the movies on Wednesday night. The honor roll students would be allowed to go to the movies every Wednesday night during the Florida term rather than attending study hall.

One thing that did not immediately change with the end of the war was the necessity for young men to register for the draft. Captain O. O. Pillans, affectionately known as OOP to the cadets, requested that those students who had recently celebrated their eighteenth birthday give him their names. Once he had the cadets' names, he would write letters requesting deferments. He informed those cadets who needed to register for the draft that they could do so at Wimmers Real Estate Office next to the Gulf Theater in Venice. In previous years, cadets had to travel to Sarasota to register. Captain Pillans urged those senior who planned on going to college to submit their applications early. He was concerned that many colleges would fill their admission quotes quickly because of the number of returning veterans applying for admission.

The cadets were scheduled to participate in two-pageant parades during the Florida term. In February, the band went to Fort Myers to march in the Edison Pageant of Light.

Cadets March in the Pageant of Sara de Sota—Venice

Although no announcement was made as to the best band in the parade, many said that KMI ranked among the best. Later in the month, the entire battalion, along with 18 other bands and 221 floats, was scheduled to march in the Pageant of Sara de Sota. However, after the battalion assembled in full dress uniforms in front of the San Marco, Major Hodgin announced that the corps would not be going to Sarasota. Apparently, because of some sort of misunderstanding, no buses had been sent from Sarasota to pick up the cadets. As a result, the cadets were free to spend the night in normal Saturday night activities. The Anvil reported that a number of cadets somehow managed to get to Sarasota to enjoy the festivities associated with the pageant.

Two weeks after the canceled trip to the Sara de Sota Pageant, the cadets learned that the Sarasota Chamber of Commerce was sponsoring a trip to see the Boston Red Sox play the Detroit Tigers. The trip to Sarasota would be made by buses furnished by the chamber. The trip was being sponsored by Joe Cronin, the manager of the Red Sox, and was to compensate the cadets for the failure to furnish transportation to the pageant. Admission to the game was free, as was transportation to and from Sarasota.

In March of 1946, Lt. Col. H. E. Dooley, Professor of Military Science and Tactics, announced that the KMI rifle team had won the William Randolph Hearst Trophy for the second straight year in the Junior Military School Division. He announced that KMI beat every other university, military school, and high school, a total of fifty-four teams, in the Fifth Service Command. The Fifth Service Command included schools in Kentucky, Ohio, West Virginia, and Indiana. Only Culver Military Academy, a senior unit, was excluded because it was a senior unit and competed only with universities.[206]

One interesting class that was started in the mid-1940s was called Physical Training but was more commonly known as posture class. The class was composed of eight cadets from each company. The cadets were chosen by their company commanders and platoon leaders because they needed posture training. The classes were held twice a week during the drill periods. Cadets remained in the class until the instructors thought they no longer needed the training.[207]

In 1946, the annual Government Inspection was held immediately before the school returned to Kentucky. On Sunday afternoon, March 31, a full review and inspection was held by the review board. Following the review, Company B performed a close order drill exhibition. On Monday,

---

[206] The *Kayemeye Anvil*, Vol. II, No. 19, March 3, 1946.
[207] The *Kayemeye Anvil*, Vol. IV, No. 6, Oct 26, 1947.

various practical tests were given, and an attack and defense problem was held. On Tuesday morning, various theoretical tests were given before the board left. On Wednesday morning, the corps boarded the KMI Special and returned to Kentucky.

The annual practice of awarding prizes for outstanding performance during Government Inspection was modified in 1946. Only awards were given for best rooms on each stoop. The occupants of the best room on each stoop received $5, to be divided between the room's occupants. The second place room on each stoop received $3. For 1946, the occupants of the best room on each stoop would receive an extra day of leave for spring vacation.

Les Brown's band was selected for the commencement dance. The cost for the band would be about $1,400. That meant that the seniors would be assessed $6 apiece and the juniors $5. The cadets were advised to write home for their money because a deposit was necessary to reserve the band. Undoubtedly, Mrs. Crutcher's "End of the Season" dance was more popular with most of the cadets because the price was much more reasonable. The dance was free to members of the dance class and only fifty cents for nonmembers. Captain Stutzenburger's school orchestra, the Kampus Kats, provided the music for the dance which was attended by almost half of the corps.

The 1945-1946 school year ended with the graduation of sixty-two seniors and fourteen Junior School cadets.

November 1947, the cadet corps participated in Louisville's Armistice Day Parade. The corps was taken to the downtown assembly area in Louisville by bus. The previous year, the corps had won the award for the best unit in the parade, and they hoped to repeat that performance.[208]

In the fall of 1947, the KMI football team went undefeated with a 9—0 record. It was the first time since the 1941 that the team was undefeated. Following the regular season, they played St. Xavier in Lexington in a game sponsored by the Olcika Shrine Temple. The charity game was played at Stoll Field in Lexington on Thanksgiving Day. The game had originally started in 1938 as an East-West all-star game, but it had been changed during World War II to a game between the best high school teams available. The KMI and St. Xavier teams usually met during

---

[208]   The *Kayemeye Anvil*, Vol. IV, No. 8, November 9, 1947.

the regular season, but because of schedule conflicts, they did not play in 1947.

The St. X team was ranked number 3 in the state while KMI was ranked number 5. This ranking was despite the fact that St. X was 6 and 3 while KMI was 9—0. Despite a muddy field, the cadets ran their record to 10—0 by defeating St. Xavier by the score of 13—0. It was the second postseason game for the cadets. The first game had been the Celery Bowl played in Florida at a much earlier date.[209]

The KMI basketball team took a three-year winning streak into the 1948 season. The streak came to an end on February 17, 1948, when the Sarasota Sailors defeated the cadets by a score of 50 to 48. The forty game-winning streak was the longest in school history.[210]

In 1948, KMI participated in the Edison Pageant of Light Parade in Fort Meyers by sending the band, the color guard, and selected cadet officers. The corps also furnished an honor guard for the crowning of the king and queen of the Sara de Sota Pageant, and the entire corps of cadets participated in the pageant's parade.

The corps returned to Kentucky in 1948, not on a special train, but aboard four cars attached to the Southland train. The change was made because there was a coal strike, and the railroad would not make a special train available to transport the school. The cadets were happy with the new arrangement because the early departure of the Southland meant that they received an extra day of spring vacation. When the cadets returned from their break, they found that the dugout had been redecorated, and further renovations were planned.

In the fall of 1948, two new members of the faculty were William T. Simpson and George Bales. Simpson was a veteran of the navy and

Cadets Form Honor Guard for King and Queen of the Sara de Sota Pageant—McDonald

---

[209] The *Kayemeye Anvil* Vol. IV, No. 11, Nov 30, 1947.
[210] The *Kayemeye Anvil* Vol. IV, No. 20, Feb 22 1948.

a graduate of Davidson College. He would hold a number of positions at KMI before becoming superintendent in 1965. He was, at various times, an instructor of mathematics, coach of the junior varsity and varsity basketball teams, director of admissions, secretary of the alumni association, and assistant to the president and coordinator of instruction. He would earn a master's degree from the University of Louisville and a PhD Degree from the University of Kentucky. Bales, who was a graduate of Hampton-Sydney College, was, at various times, an instructor of Latin I and II, economics, government, and psychology. He was also the coach of the tennis team, the junior varsity basketball team, and the freshman football team.

Chapter VII

---•---

THE GOLDEN YEARS

The one thing that was fairly consistent throughout KMI's history was the rapid involvement of the new cadets in the activities of the school. In 1955, for instance, new cadets were instructed to arrive between 10:00 a.m. and 6:00 p.m. on Monday, September 12. "A program of orientation will begin at 7:00 p.m. that evening and will continue through September 14. Classes will begin on Thursday, September 15. The new student should bring from home only those items listed in the school catalog. The new cadet should bring only the civilian clothes which he wore to school. As soon as he arrives he will be fitted with a light weight uniform and will have no occasion to wear civilian clothes here at any time during the school year."[211] To greet the new cadets, there were members of the faculty and a few cadet officers. The first days were filled with various aptitude tests, the issuing of textbooks, decisions to be made about classes, and, of course, the issuance of uniforms.

The school administration would have preferred that new cadets arrive without their parents, thereby eliminating long and, in some cases, tearful goodbyes. "Parents should not accompany their sons to school on opening day. Long experience has taught us that it is much better for the development of a cadet's self-reliance for him to be on his own from the time he arrives at the school."[212] Most new cadets arrived with the civilian

---

[211] O. O. Pillans, "To Parents of New Cadets of Kentucky Military Institute," 1955-56, July 21, 1955.

[212] To the New Patrons of the Kentucky Military Institute, 1955-56 Session, August 9, 1955.

clothes on their back and a duffel bag or suitcase filled with items that the school recommended they bring with them. The hectic activity of the first few days was designed to keep the cadets busy and hopefully prevent the onset of homesickness. There were always a few cadets who battled homesickness for a few days or a few weeks.[213]

The new cadets who brought only a few articles other than those suggested by the school watched in amazement as the old cadets unloaded their belongings. Such things as radios, record players, tape recorders, small portable televisions, golf clubs, and other sports equipment were carried into the barracks. Rather than a duffel bag, footlockers emerged from the cars, and it soon became clear to the New Boys that they had a lot to learn about what to bring to school.

A major adjustment for most of the new cadets was the lack of friends. If he knew any other cadets, they were probably Old Boys, and they would not associate with Rats. One former cadet related that someone from his hometown was a cadet, and he expected him to be a friend. On their first encounter after the new cadet arrived, his hometown friend handed him two toothbrushes and sent him off to clean the toilets on their stoop. If the new cadet was not outgoing and did not make friends easily, his first days could be very lonely. He no longer had the support of his family and friends that he had known all his life. Although he now lived in a highly structured environment, he was, for all intents and purposes, on his own. Some cadets adjusted quickly, others took longer, and some were unable to cope with

Mail Call—Young

the new situation. Those who could not adapt might leave during the year or not return after completing their first year.

---

[213]   The school recommended that each new Cadet bring with them: three soft white shirts with collar and cuffs attached; six suits of underwear; eight pairs of black socks; four pairs of pajamas; one pair of tennis shoes; one pair bathing trunks; one bathrobe; one pair bathroom slippers; six bath towels; one pair black shoes, plain toes; one pillow; three pillow cases; three pair of sheets for single bed; twelve handkerchiefs; two laundry bags; one sewing kit; one rug, optional; and toilet articles.

The amount of contact most cadets had with family and friends was limited to letters and occasional phone calls. If it was necessary, the school switchboard operator would place telephone calls to a cadet's parents, but only during free periods. The cadets could also receive calls through the switchboard from their parents. In Lyndon, there were telephone booths next to the Edison Science building that the cadets could use to make calls. Getting access to the phone booths was difficult because there were usually lines of cadets waiting to make calls to their girlfriends in the surrounding towns. The phones were the busiest following evening study hall when cadets made a mad dash to the phones. Once a phone was in use, it was almost impossible, short of threats of physical violence, to get the cadet to give up the phone so someone else could make a call. One former cadet related that some of the cadets resorted to removing the speakers from the handset so that only he could receive and make calls. He reported that the more resourceful cadets quickly raided telephone booths in the Louisville area for speakers so that they could access the phones on campus. He was also able to remember, after more than fifty years, that one of the phone numbers was TWinbrook 3-3065.

For many of the cadets, mail call was the most anticipated event of the day. Letters and care packages from home were welcomed by the cadets, especially packages that contained food items. Perhaps the most important letters were those from friends from home, especially girlfriends. For those cadets who received little or no mail, mail call must have been the most depressing time of the day.

Another adjustment the new cadet had to make was to the fact that there was a total lack of privacy. He might have shared a room with a brother, but now he shared a room with two or three people who initially were complete strangers. If the cadet was the least bit modest, he had to adjust to the fact that the showers were completely open bays and the toilet stalls had no doors. Since everyone was on the same schedule, virtually everyone was trying to shower and use the bathroom facilities at the same time. One former cadet related that at first, one of his roommates did not undress until after lights out. After about a month, he finally started getting ready for bed like everyone else in the room.

The first few days were not only filled with endless activity but a certain amount of confusion. The New Boys had been dropped into a totally new environment that required a tremendous amount of adjustment on their part. The first adjustment was the fact that life was now regulated by bugle calls, "What does that mean?" was a constant question. Other lessons to be learned came at the new cadets with dizzying speed. How to properly make a bed; how to polish brass; how to shine shoes; when to speak and when not to speak; who to salute and who not to salute; how to stand at attention properly; eventually, how to fieldstrip and clean his rifle; and countless other things that had never occurred to him before. The new cadets also encountered an entirely new vocabulary: floors of buildings were now stoops; bathrooms were sinks; stick meant a report for misconduct; SNS meant his shoes were not shined; SWOP, sinks without permission, meant he had not sought permission to visit the bathroom during times cadets were to be in their rooms; and other equally strange statements. The new cadet became familiar with such things as button boards, collar stays, military tucks for shirts, no boats in hats, and when to wear his hat. Perhaps the most notable change was the regulation haircut, any cadet whose hair was too long quickly learned the location of the barbershop.

The cadets learned how to arrange their clothes in their dressers, how to hang uniform parts in the closet in the proper order, arranging books according to their height, and, in later years, learning their laundry number. All cadets were told to have name tags sewn in their clothes when they came to school, but he was also assigned a laundry number upon arrival. The first digits indicated the new cadet's alphabetical ranking among the new cadets, and the final digit was the year he had entered. The cadet having the number 123-4 would have been the 123rd new cadet admitted in 1954 or 1964. The laundry number would be used to identify clothes, textbooks, and any other personal items that it could be printed on.

The New Boys or Rats were greeted by a group of cadet officers who were responsible for getting some sort of organization done before the rest of the cadet corps arrived. Much of the activity was observed by members of the football team who were present for early practice. The observers must have wondered if the disorganized Rats would ever become acceptable cadets.

The issuing of uniform items brought the new cadet face to face with "Kappy" Kapfhammer, who was the school quartermaster. Kappy had been issuing uniforms for years and could almost guess what size items a cadet wore. If the cadet protested that the items were too tight or too big, Kappy's answer was "You'll lose some weight" or "You'll grow into them." One surprise awaiting the new cadets was the fact that there were no side pockets in their uniform pants. Some cadets would have pockets added to the pants, but most cadets learned to live without any side pockets. After the cadet had his clothing items, he took them to an area, for a number of years, the library in Ormsby Hall, where a group of women measured pants and blouses and then altered them. This was probably the busiest place on campus for the first few weeks of the school year. In addition to altering the new uniforms, the women also sewed on stripes for all the cadets who had been promoted and altered the uniforms of the old cadets who had outgrown their uniforms over the summer months.

Once the new cadets received their uniforms and they were altered, at least the corps had the appearance of a military organization until it had to move as a unit. Until the new cadets learned the basic fundamentals of close order drill, there was confusion in the ranks. For several weeks, there were people who could not remember their right from their left. Those cadets would become accustomed to someone yelling at them, sometimes from a distance, but frequently up close and very personal. When the entire student body was finally on campus, life settled down into a routine that had been followed, with little variation, by cadets for generations. Classes were small, and there was ample opportunity for individual recitation. But the course content was a little different than what the students would have received in their previous schools.

The first few weeks of afternoon drill were filled with mistakes and a lot of shouting at the new cadets. There was one particular danger in the drill sessions, learning the manual of arms with rifles. For a number of years, the cadets had used the 03 Springfield rifle; but at some point, they were issued the M1 Garand.

The M1 had been the standard infantry weapon during World War II and the Korean War. The rifle weighed approximately 9.5 pounds empty. The cadets were required to perform inspection arms. The first movement required the cadet to push the handle of the operating rod toward the butt of the rifle with his left hand. This operation would lock the bolt in the open position. At the command "Port Arms," it was necessary to place the heel of the right hand on the handle of the operating rod and depress the follower located inside the rifle with the right thumb. Once the follower was depressed, the cadet quickly removed the heel of his hand from the handle of the operating rod. If the cadet did not perform this maneuver quickly and properly, a strong spring slammed the bolt shut, catching the thumb of the right hand. It was not uncommon during the first weeks of school to see cadets with swollen black thumbs, "M1 Thumb," walking around campus.

The first few weeks passed fairly quickly. New cadets learned how to use items such as Brasso, Blitz Cloths, collar stays, and button boards. They learned how to tie a necktie, *no* Windsor knots, wear their uniform properly, and arrange their clothes in the closet and dresser drawers. They learned how to fieldstrip and clean their M1 rifle and memorize its serial number. They quickly found out who was to be addressed as "sir" and who was not. They learned to listen for the announcement following reveille call, after the public address system was installed, of the uniform of the day.

Meals were served family style, and most cadets learned to eat what was served because there was no place to get anything else to eat other than light snacks. One former cadet, when asked what he remembered most about KMI, answered, "Always being hungry!" All cadets were assigned seats in the dining room. A faculty member sat at one end of the table and a ranking cadet at the other end. The tables were usually divided in half, and the individuals at the head and foot were responsible for their half of the table. The food was brought to the individuals at the head and foot of the table, and they served themselves and then passed the food to his right around his half of the table. The individual who sat to his left was sitting in "Starvation Corner." The person at the head of the table was the only person who was allowed to talk the waiters during the meal.

The meals were served by cadet waiters who were working to earn spending money or help defray the cost of attending KMI. The waiters also served as go-betweens for cadets trading food items. A cadet who did not like a particular item, poached eggs for instance, could trade that item to another cadet for something he liked, perhaps a particular kind of meat or dessert. The amount of food served was not abundant but was probably adequate for most of the cadets. The one exception was in Florida. If cadets were lucky enough to sit at a table with a good fisherman, he could expect to eat a lot of fresh fish. Any cadet who brought in a large catch could have it cleaned and cooked for his table. The cooks kept any extra fish for themselves and usually returned to Kentucky with an ample supply of frozen fish.

Cadets quickly learned to budget their money. Following a policy that had been in place throughout most of the school's history, parents placed money in an account with the school for their sons. The money would then be distributed weekly to the cadets in an amount designated by the parents. Allowance day was important for most of the cadets, and a long line quickly formed when it was time for the money to be distributed. For necessities, haircuts, school supplies, and personal grooming products, the cadets could sign requisition slips at the quartermaster store and the dugout. At the end of each month, the requisition slips were totaled, and a bill was sent to the parents. For all other expenses, the cadets were dependent upon their allowance, the occasional money sent from home, or money they might have earned, either at school or at home.

In Kentucky, other than the weekly trips to Louisville on the day off, there were few ways to spend allowance money. Some cadets would walk to Lyndon to buy food items at the small grocery store or visit the small drugstore. The cadets often purchased canned foods that they could heat in their rooms. Most cadets either owned a hot plate or a Sterno stove or knew where they could borrow something to heat canned foods. Although hot plates were prohibited because of the load they placed on the electrical system, they were available. Some enterprising cadets in the late 1950s and early 1960s had hamburgers and french fries delivered by taxi from restaurants in St. Matthews. The most popular items were ranch burgers. The cadets not only made money on the operation, but they also got to eat free hamburgers. There always seemed to be a ready market for such deliveries, even when the dugout tried selling small hamburgers and hot dogs.

I Think It's Done—Brinker

The dugout, operated by Mr. Scoggins for many years and located in the basement of A Barracks along with the barbershop, was the only place on the Lyndon campus where cadets could spend their money. Various personal grooming items were available: shaving cream, razor blades, and butch wax for example, which the cadet could sign requisition slips to pay for the purchase. Just like the requisitions signed at the quartermaster store, the student's purchases were totaled and the bill sent to the parents each month. Other items, such as candy bars, potato chips, and sodas could be purchased by the cadets. One item that was purchased by many cadets was a milk card.

The card allowed the cadet to purchase quarter pint containers of milk without spending any of their limited cash. Many of the cadets had a letter on file that allowed them to purchase an unlimited number of milk cards during the year, and it was not unusual to see cadets purchasing four or five containers of milk. At various times, the seniors laid claim to one area of the dugout for their exclusive use, and it was a sorry nonsenior who strayed into their area.

Also located in the basement of A Barracks was the barbershop. There were usually two barbers available to cut hair during the morning hours. Cadets needing haircuts would sign out at the guardhouse during their vacant class period and go to the barbershop. Only two cadets per barber were allowed in the area at any one time. A member of the guard detail would periodically check the barbershop to make sure that the number of cadets did not exceed the limit and that those cadets who were signed out to the barbershop were actually getting their hair cut. In Venice, the cadets went to a local barbershop. The cadets paid for their haircuts by signing a requisition slip.

The situation in Venice was completely different. There were numerous places where the cadets would spend their money. There was the drugstore just across the drill field, there was a convenient grocery store, restaurants, and, in later years, the Dairy Queen. For those cadets who had boats, the expenses would have been higher to cover the

Cadets in the Venice Drugstore—McDonald

cost of gas and oil. However, they had the advantage of being able to take to the water whenever they had free time. At times, cadets would pool their money and charter a deep sea fishing boat. At other times, cadets would rent a boat and spend a day fishing and swimming in various rivers and bays. When their money was short or nonexistent, there was always the beach. Some of the cadets used their time on the beach to supplement their allowance while still enjoying the sun and surf. Venice billed itself as the "Sharks' Tooth Capital," and the cadets could find the teeth by walking along the beach and then sell them to the various shops in town.

Bob Briner, who owned and operated the Dairy Queen for more than forty-five years and was affectionately known to the cadets as "Dairy Queen Bob," always made certain that the hungry cadets received very generous servings of anything they ordered. The Dairy Queen, along with the drugstore across the street from the San Marco, were popular gathering places for the cadets during their free time.

Cadets Relax at the Dairy Queen—Brinker

The transition to life in Florida was not difficult. About all that really changed were the scenery and the weather. The daily activities were the same until the afternoon recreation period. Instead of being confined to the ninety-six-acre campus, there was the beach, boating, and fishing as well as organized sports. Each year there were a few cadets who refused to heed the warnings about the results of too much exposure to sun, sand, and water. One or two seriously sunburned cadets, a few requiring a stay in the infirmary, convinced everyone to be careful. One thing that all of the cadets remembered about the first weeks in Florida was the constant aggravation caused by sandspurs. The small thorny burs seemed to be everywhere and attached themselves to socks and pants until enough cadets had tramped through the grass to collect them all. The sharp spikes on the burs were painful and not easy to remove. The problem was most painful when marching because there was no opportunity to stop and remove the offending burs.

Just as Colonels Fowler and Richmond liked to tell everyone, the health of the cadets in Florida was generally excellent. The infirmary saw relatively few cadets, and most of those visits were the result of sports injuries. At some point, school officials arranged for an insurance policy to cover the

Cadets Head for a Day on the Water—Venice

cadets. The policy began with the start of the school year and continued through summer vacation. The plan covered "all accidents (including sports) whether sustained at school, at home or while traveling, or wherever the student may be." The policy included the following: "physicians', surgeons', and nurses' fees, hospital, laboratory, and x-ray costs, medicines, and, in short, any medical costs incurred as the result of an accident. Reimbursement will be made up to a limit of $500 in any one case." The cost of the policy was $15 a year.[214]

Under Colonel Richmond's administration, KMI maintained an infirmary in both Kentucky and Florida. In Kentucky, the infirmary was located in Fowler Hall and could accommodate about ten cadets. The infirmary in Florida was also located in the Junior School building between the Venice and San Marco. For a number of years, the school nurse was Evelyn "Maw" Fowler, who was no relation to Colonel Fowler, who treated minor ailments. Each morning, a local doctor paid a visit to the school to attend to the more seriously ill cadets. Cadets who believed they needed medical attention could report to sick call each morning. In the event of serious illnesses and injuries, the cadet would be sent to one of the local hospitals.

One policy that the school implemented at some point that provided a break from school routine for some cadets was the granting of weekend leaves during both the fall and winter terms. The leaves were granted "to a cadet only for the purpose of spending time with his parents or with a close relative of mature age." As a safeguard against

KENTUCKY MILITARY INSTITUTE

Lyndon, Kentucky—Venice, Florida

Application   Approved
           Disapproved

Signed ....

Reported Departure at

_____   _____
(Time)   (Date)

Reported Return at

_____   _____
(Time)   (Date)

Signed..
              Officer of the Day

Leave Slip—Young

---

[214] Undated letter to patrons of Kentucky Military Institute.

enterprising cadets who might try to circumvent the system, "Requests for such weekends should be addressed to the Commandant in writing by the parents. Telegrams and telephone calls are not acceptable." The request for leave had to be received by Thursday before the desired weekend leave. No cadet was allowed to take another cadet on leave with his family.

The weekend leaves were granted only to those cadets who were in good standing. That meant he had passed all academic work for the previous month and had a total of eight merits. Leave began after drill on the last day of classes for the week and ended at 7:00 p.m. on the day before classes resumed. Many cadets took advantage of the weekend leave policy, especially when parents came to visit in Florida. Those cadets who did not take weekend leave during the fall term were allowed to leave one day early at Christmas. Those who did not take leave in Florida were allowed to return one day late at the end of spring vacation.[215]

The one break in the tightly controlled routine came on the day off. Whether it came on a Saturday or Monday, the day was greeted with anticipation by those cadets who were not confined to campus or walking penalty tours. On the day off, there was a major room inspection following breakfast. Following the inspection, cadets who lived near the school could sign out to go home, and other cadets could accompany them home. In Kentucky, many of the cadets went to Louisville for the day, provided they had money to finance a day in town. In the 1950s and '60s, buses transported the cadets to downtown Louisville; prior to that, the cadets had taken the interurban that stopped across from the front gate.

Ready for Inspection—Tullis

Those cadets who went to Louisville spent the day at the movies, visiting various stores, and finding some place to eat that they could afford. In some cases, they might visit the YMCA to play a

---

[215] Letter on Christmas vacation and weekend leave, 1959; undated Blue Book, Item 96, paragraph B and C, p. 21.

few games of pool. Chester Travelstead, KMI 1929, described a Monday in Louisville, which was not much different than that enjoyed by cadets three decades later. He ate an inexpensive meal at a White Castle, went to a number of different stores, and simply relaxed. The one thing he did that was a little unusual was to spend some time in the lobby of the Seelbach Hotel, watching people.[216]

Those cadets who lived close to the campus could go home for the day and take fellow cadets with them. The only requirement was that a parent pick the cadets up at school and bring them back by the required time in the evening. Those cadets who were lucky enough to be able to go home quickly changed out of their uniforms and for the day resumed a fairly normal lifestyle. Perhaps the best part of the day was a good and plentiful meal. The cadets who went to Louisville wore their uniforms and were readily identifiable and had to be on their best behavior. Conduct away from campus was subject to the same rules and punishments as on campus. The Blue Book stipulated that "any cadet who shall, when absent from the school, commit any act reflecting on the good name of the Corps of cadets may be punished as if the act had been committed on the Campus."[217]

One event that was a standard practice throughout the twentieth century was laundry day. There are photographs of cadets from the early 1900s lined up in front of Ormsby Hall and the barracks with their laundry bags beside them. Each week, the cadets brought their dirty laundry to morning formation where the bags were collected and taken to a commercial laundry. After about a week, the clean clothes were returned. New cadets were probably surprised to find that their shirts and pants contained a significant amount of starch. The cadets frequently joked that their pants could stand up by themselves. The cost of a predetermined amount of laundry was included in the cost of tuition. The parents of

A 1910 Laundry Formation—Venice

---

[216] "No School on Monday," http://www.unm.edu/~ddarling/v6v8s1.html.
[217] Undated Blue Book, Article 66.

those cadets who exceeded the standard amount of dirty clothing would receive a bill each month to cover the cost of the additional laundry.

On May 25, 1952, the entire cadet corps, in full dress uniforms, boarded buses for a trip to the Fourth Avenue Presbyterian Church in downtown Louisville. The occasion was the marriage of Diane Richmond, Colonel Richmond's daughter, to William T. Simpson. Following the ceremony, Mr. and Mrs. Simpson left the church through an archway of crossed sabers formed by an honor guard of cadet officers. The cadets returned to Lyndon, where they were treated to cake and punch in the dining room.[218]

At some point in the 1950s, a building was constructed at the far end of the school's property behind the gymnasium. The building was apparently the idea of Captain O. O. Pillans, who served as the secretary of the alumni association. He believed that the association needed a dedicated place to hold its meetings when they were held in Lyndon. The idea was expanded to allow the facility to be used as a clubhouse for members of the senior class. By using it as a clubhouse, the building would not be unused for most of the year and it would provide the seniors the opportunity to escape some of the

Mr. and Mrs. William T. Simpson and Cadet Honor Guard—Simpson

rigid rules and regulations of the school. Who actually paid for the building, it can be assumed that the Alumni Association paid for all or a portion of the cost, is lost to history. Eventually, the senior clubhouse would become a refuge for seniors during their free hours. The building had a pool table, a console television, a Coke machine and lots of chairs and couches. The seniors held class meetings in the clubhouse as well as dances and other social events. The alumni association would hold their

---

[218] William T. Simpson to the author, November 22, 2012.

meetings in the clubhouse when they held meeting at homecoming and other times.[219]

The 1952 Catalog contained an assertion that was reminiscent of Colonel Fowler's "Not a Reform School" statement:

Three Seniors Clean the Clubhouse—Young

> If a boy is inclined to be unruly, or if he cannot be trusted, we do not wish to have him apply for admission. There has been a mistaken impression on the part of the public, which, happily, is dying out, that a military school is a place for the detention or reformation of bad boys. The personnel of our student body is as fine as that of any non-military school in the country, and we will not knowingly enroll a boy of vicious habits.[220]

The catalog went on to lay out some general rules that were to be observed by all cadets:

> No student may use alcohol in any form, and immediate dismissal will result after the first offense. No cadet may keep a motorcycle or automobile on or near campus. No cadet may damage or mutilate property without making an immediate settlement. No cadet may keep civilian clothes on the campus after he has received his uniform. No cadet shall engage in gambling of any kind. No cadet may engage in any form of hazing. No cadet shall use obscene or profane language. No cadet shall have firearms in his possession. Every cadet will be required to write a letter home every Sunday night. Every cadet

---

[219] E-mail, William T. Simpson to the author, March 18, 2013.
[220] Catalog 1952-1953, p. 62.

will be fully informed of the rules and regulations of the school through the "Blue Book."[221]

Students who needed extra work on their mathematic studies could take advantage of a summer camp that Colonel Sam Marshall conducted at his farm in Mingo, West Virginia. The students at the Circle-O-Ranch received work in the areas where they had weaknesses. In addition, they had the opportunity to ride horses and hike through the countryside. They also perform various tasks that needed to be done around the farm. From all accounts, most of the boys enjoyed the time they spent with the Marshals in West Virginia. For several years, Diane Simpson ran a day camp on the KMI campus. Known as Country Day Camp, but more commonly known as the KMI Day Camp, there were two sessions of four weeks. The students were transported by buses to and from the campus each day. The young attendees participated in a variety of activities during the day including swimming, basketball, and learning to play golf. One camper reported that about the only coed activity was swimming. The students ate lunch in the dining hall and good manners were emphasized.[222] The camp employed a number of high school students from Louisville to assist with the young campers.

---

[221] Catalog 1952-1953, p. 62.
[222] E-mail from W.T. Simpson to the author, March 19, 2013.

Chapter VIII

Change Arrives in a Pontiac Convertible

In October 1953, change was on the way to KMI in a new Pontiac convertible. Newly promoted Major Donald A. Seibert was on his way to Lyndon to assume the duties of professor of Military Science and Tactics (PMS&T). The major, a decorated combat veteran of World War II and Korea, was not pleased with his assignment and had twice tried to have it changed. The first time he had appealed to Major General James C. Fry, the Chief of Infantry. General Fry informed Seibert that he had personally selected him for the assignment to

Major Donald A. Seibert,
PMS&T—Young

KMI. The army felt that there were problems with the ROTC program at KMI, and General Fry believed that the major was the person to correct those problems. Although he had heard the order, Seibert still refused to accept the decision as final.

During a visit to Fort Bragg, he met with Major General Joseph P. Cleland, the XVIII Airborne Corps commander. When General Cleland discovered that Seibert was unhappy with his assignment, he called General Fry and requested that the major be assigned as his aide. General

Fry informed General Cleland that orders could not be changed to satisfy individual officers. With that, Seibert reluctantly accepted the fact that he was going to Lyndon, Kentucky.[223]

In an interview with retired Colonel Seibert years later, he still questioned the assignment. He did not feel that he was temperamentally suited to deal with high school and junior school cadets. When pushed about the assignment, the colonel stated that he felt that it might be a career-ending assignment. A posting as a professor of Military Science and Tactics at a college or university was not necessarily good for an officer's career, but an assignment to a high school was definitely worse.

Major Seibert's first dealings with Colonel Richmond were strained. Colonel Richmond, probably aware of Seibert's instructions, did not meet with the major for several days after his arrival in Lyndon. When they finally did meet, Colonel Richmond indicated that he expected the major to follow the practices of his predecessors. Seibert, mindful of his instructions from General Fry, replied that he would determine what was needed in the military training of the cadets. He expressed the hope that the two would be able to work out any problems on a satisfactory basis.[224]

Colonel Richmond then made a demand that still angered Seibert fifty years after the fact. The colonel stated that he did not drink and neither did the faculty at KMI. He made it clear that he expected that Seibert and the members of the Military Department would also abstain. The major informed Richmond that the members of the military detachment would not drink on campus and would not attend to their duties after drinking. But under no circumstances would he order them to abstain. The major indicated that if the colonel did not like his answer, he could request his reassignment. Colonel Seibert noted in his memoirs, *The Regulars: An Account of the Military Career of Colonel Donald A. Seibert, USA Ret*, that "we departed shortly, not too amicably. This is the way our relation remained throughout my tenure. We were studiously courteous to each other, but there was no cordiality between us." With this less than auspicious beginning, Major Seibert began what would be three years filled with sweeping changes. The first change was in the practices

---

[223] Donald A. Seibert, *The Regulars: An Account of the Military Career of Colonel Donald A. Seibert*, hereafter cited as Seibert, p. 237.

[224] Seibert, op. cit., pp. 239-240.

followed during afternoon drill sessions. Major Seibert observed that there was a great deal of standing around and socializing and very little drilling. He took immediate steps to increase the amount of time the cadets were actively involved in drilling.[225]

A more significant change was the closing of the outdoor small bore firing range. The range had been in use for a number of years, but a survey indicated that it was unsafe even for .22 caliber rifles. The Military Department developed a plan that would bring the range into compliance with existing safety standards. However, the plan required the expenditure of funds by the school for reconstructing the range. Colonel Richmond declined to make the funds available, and Seibert closed the range. Fortunately, he was able to make arrangements for the use of the firing range at a local National Guard armory, and the rifle team was able to practice and fire its matches.[226]

After the move to Venice and the first Sunday parade, Major Seibert found himself in a serious conflict with Colonel Richmond. The Sunday parades were extremely popular and drew large crowds. However, the major considered them to be decidedly unmilitary and filled with nonmilitary gimmicks. When he announced to the cadets that the parades would assume a more military form, he was called to the colonel's office.

Colonel Richmond argued that the parades were important to the school, and he was concerned that changing the

Spectators at a Sunday Parade—Morgan

format would diminish attendance. Seibert made his position clear: "COL Richmond, you are not running a carnival. You are running a military school. These cadets are supposed to be learning proper military drill. I cannot countenance military formations being made into circuses. There are many interesting and different parades that we will use, but they will

---

[225] Seibert, op. cit., pp. 238 and 240.
[226] Seibert, op. cit., pp. 241-242.

be authorized formations. There is nothing more stirring than a well drilled military unit. We will put on a fine performance, but it will be a military one." Colonel Richmond relented, and the parade format was changed. The changes proved to be popular with the public, and they remained in place long after the major left KMI.[227]

One of the most popular decisions made by the new PMS&T was the one that established the Kentucky Rifles. The school did not have a drill team, and the major believed that it would be popular and would encourage all of the cadets to improve their drill. The Military Department obtained M1903 Springfield rifles from the army. A distinctive uniform

St. Valentine's Day Parade—Morgan

was developed from uniform items that the cadets already owned, and the forty members of the team were selected. Cadet Lt. Joe Gandolfo was selected as the commander of the new unit. Gandolfo drilled the team until they executed their maneuvers flawlessly. From their first performance at a Sunday parade in Venice, the Kentucky Rifles were extremely popular not only with the spectators, but also with the cadet corps. The Kentucky Rifles participated as a unit in the various parades in Florida, such as the Fort Myers Edison Pageant of Light. Special parade routines were developed so that the team could perform without delaying the progress of the parade. As with their Sunday performances, the Kentucky Rifles were always extremely popular at the various pageants. Some of the movements that the Kentucky Rifles performed to the delight of the crowds were the following: Ripple to the Rear, Venice Move, Vee Formation, Kentucky Move, Circle Formation, and the Queen Ann's Salute.[228]

In the summer of 1954, the Military Department prepared a Standard Operating Procedure (SOP) to be used by the cadets to govern their

---

227   Seibert, op. cit., pp. 242-243.
228   Seibert, op. cit., pp. 244-245.

military activities. The *Kentucadet* described the SOP as a booklet that outlined "the object of the R.O.T.C. program, the organization of the Cadet Corps, the traditions of the school, and the scope of the military training program. It contains circulars covering uniforms, awards and decorations, weapons and government equipment, and military courtesy and etiquette. All the parade and inspection procedures are outlined also." Nothing like the SOP had existed before, and it standardized many of the military practices and provided a guide to all the military rules. For instances, it provided clear guidelines for how awards and decorations were to be worn on the uniform, thus standardizing the appearance of the cadets' uniforms.[229]

The First Kentucky Rifles—Arrowood

Other new ideas were adopted during the 1954-1955 school year. The most significant of these changes was that cadets were to salute all officers. This apparently caused some problems until the old cadets adjusted to the new practice. Another new practice was the institution of a reveille formation. Not very popular with the cadets, it was designed to get everyone out of bed and in uniform in ten minutes. As the *Kentucadet* reported, "The boys still straggle to formation but at least everyone is up for inspection and soupee." Another lasting innovation made during the 1954-1955 school year was the creation of the Military Police Squad by M/Sgt. E. A. Rusteri of the Military Department. The primary purpose of the squad was to direct traffic during

The Military Police Squad—Young

---

[229] Seibert, op. cit., pp. 247 and 250; The *Kentucadet*, Vol. XXX, No. 2, December 1954, p. 6.

special events, such as Parent's Day, Homecoming, Mother's Day, and the parades in Venice. Dressed in a distinctive uniform, the MPs attended all parades as the color guard.[230]

On January 31, 1955, Colonel Richmond sent a letter to the alumni requesting their help in recruiting prospective students. He stated that under his and Colonel Hodgin's administration, the number of students had grown from 167 to 331. He attributed the growth to the strong support of the school shown by the alumni. He had sent a similar letter the previous year, as he apparently did every year, and one out of every three of the boys recommended had been admitted during the current year. He concluded by saying, "Only through the efforts of our alumni can KMI continue to keep the high place it now holds among the military schools of America."

During the 1955 Florida term, selected members of the cadet corps participated in three major pageants. The Kentucky Rifles, band, and commissioned officers went to Bradenton, Fort Myers, and Tampa. It was the first time that the school had been represented in the Tampa Gasparilla celebration since 1934.[231]

One item acquired during Major Seibert's tenure was an obsolete 105mm howitzer. An adapter which fired blank shotgun shells that was manufactured at one of the government arsenals was purchased so that the gun could be fired on ceremonial

The Canon—Young

occasions. The gun was first fired on graduation day of 1955. It was last fired at a retreat ceremony in the fall of 1956, when a member of the cadet guard detail, Thomas Jefferson (Jeff) Evans IV, was seriously injured when the adapter misfired while he was holding it in his hand. In what was perhaps an ironic twist of fate, Jeff was a color sergeant his senior year. The gun now sits silently just inside the inner gate of the old Lyndon campus, fastened to the ground, and its barrel filled with cement.[232]

---

[230]   The *Kentucadet: Alumni Journal*, Vol. XXX, No. 2, December, 1954.
[231]   The *Kentucadet: Alumni Journal*, Vol. XXX, No. 3, February 1955.
[232]   Seibert, op. cit., p. 252.

The summer of 1955 was a busy time for the Military Detachment. New lesson plans had to be developed to meet the new ROTC program of instruction (POI) and new equipment was acquired. The new equipment items that came into the school inventory were fatigues, web gear, field jackets, helmets, and shelter halves. In addition to the new individual equipment, crew-served weapons, light machine guns, and 81mm mortars became a part of the military inventory. Instruction in the use of the machine guns and mortars was incorporated into the course of instruction. The cadets were also instructed in how to live in the field. Perhaps the most frustrating part of the instruction was the proper use of the field pack and web gear. The cadets were extremely interested in the new classes since they were in preparation for the bivouac to be held in April.[233]

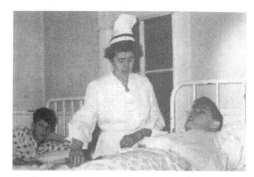

Maw Fowler and Jeff Evans—Venice

The train trip to Florida in 1956 was fairly typical of all of the trips south. The cadets boarded the KMI Special in Louisville after Christmas vacation. As the train rolled out of the station, the endless stories about Christmas vacation, the marathon card games, and reading sessions began. The train would make short stops along the way to pick up cadets who lived near the stops. Very brief stops were made in Elizabethtown, Bowling Green, Nashville, Decatur, and Birmingham, allowing just enough time for the cadets to board.

The first meal the cadets ate was served in two dining cars attached to the Special. The cadets in the chair cars moved one car at a time to the diners. The meal consisted of roast beef, green beans, mashed potatoes, rolls, milk, and ice cream. After a night of little, if any, sleep, breakfast was served in the dining cars. The train arrived in Tampa about eleven in the morning. The cadets were given about two hours to leave the train and see some of the town and eat lunch. The cadets were given money so they could buy lunch. Once the cadets returned to the Special, the final leg of

---

[233] Seibert, op. cit., p. 252.

the trip to Venice began. The cadets were greeted in Venice by the usual gathering of city officials, local citizens, including numerous young ladies and parents. Most of the cadets were able to secure rides to the San Marco, but there were an unfortunate few who had to make the walk with their luggage. Once at the San Marco, room assignments were made, and the school routine resumed with study hall.

The first Dress Parade of the year in Florida in 1956 drew an estimated crowd of four thousand. The parade was held in honor of various Venice officials, and Mayor James P. Kieron and members of the city council occupied the seats of honor. The *Kayemeye Anvil* of February 25, 1956, reported that about one hundred cadets traveled to Fort Meyers to participate in the Edison

The Welcoming Committee—Venice

Pageant of Light parade. Band Company, the officers, guidon bearers, and the Kentucky Rifles represented the school. For the second year in a row, the cadets had the honor of leading the parade which covered a two and a half mile route and passed three reviewing stands.[234]

In 1956, the KMI basketball team compiled a 12—5 record during the regular season. In the regional tournament, they defeated Lakeland and Boca Ciega but were defeated by the Jefferson High School team. Despite

Cadets Get Their Room Assignments in Venice—Venice

---

[234] *Kayemeye Anvil*, Vol. XII, No. 6, January 21, 1956; *Kayemeye Anvil*, Vol. XII, February 25, 1956.

the defeat in the regional tournament, the team moved on to the state tournament. The entire school was excited by the prospect of a Kentucky school winning the Florida state championship. However, Miami Senior High School upheld the state's honor by defeating the cadets by a score of 77—68. The Miami coach said that the KMI game was the toughest game of the tournament.

Major Seibert had one major confrontation with the cadet corps. The controversy was the result of two incidents during the winter term of 1956. The first incident occurred after the parade at the Edison Pageant of Light in Fort Meyer. Following the parade, some of the cadets were caught drinking. As a result, one officer was reduced in rank, and the others were reprimanded. The second event followed a basketball game with Venice High School at their gym. The cadets who attended the game crossed busy Highway 41, the Tamiami Trail, in a disorganized and dangerous way. The officers responsible for marching the cadets back to campus were reprimanded, and some of the privileges granted by the ROTC staff were withdrawn.[235]

A number of letters were written to the editor of the *Kayemeye Anvil* protesting the major's actions. On February 25, the *Anvil* published a long letter to the corps of cadets from Major Seibert in which he stated his disappointment in the corps:

> I cannot rationalize or condone the action of the Corps at the Venice High School under any circumstances. There can be no possible reason for such complete disregard for the instructions and orders of those in authority nor can any acceptable excuse be offered. The Corps or a large segment thereof, demonstrated complete disregard for discipline, training, courtesy, and common sense. Most of the Cadets could have found the reason for the formation if they had stopped to think—having witnessed the heedless manner in which many cadets rushed across the streets of Venice without looking out to see if any automobiles are coming. The danger of unleashing over three hundred excited cadets to cross the heavy trafficked Tamiami Trail at night should have been apparent to anyone.

---

[235] Seibert, op. cit., p. 252.

> But aside from the need for the formation, the complete lack of discipline evidence in the flagrant violation of orders indicates the necessity for additional training and greater supervision. The Corps has proved that they cannot be trusted to think or act on their own responsibility.

The major's concluding two paragraphs must have stung many of the cadets:

> In my brief tenure as PMS&T I have tried to see the cadet point of view and to accept his word and honor. It is only grudgingly that I have yielded to the constant and increasing weight of evidence that proved me wrong. I have now come to the conclusion, albeit reluctantly, that I can no longer depend upon the good faith, integrity and common sense of the Battalion. I feel that it is up to the Corps to prove in each case their intentions.
>
> I am sure the Battalion does have the sense of decency, good faith and common sense and that it is only the thoughtlessness of many of the cadets which has forced this change in my attitude. I hope that you will all make every effort to show all of the faculty that you can be trusted to act alone.

In the same issue of the paper, other letters were published that seemed to indicate that cooler heads among the cadets were beginning to prevail.

The editor of the *Anvil* wrote, "In commenting on Major Seibert's letter, one aspect should be considered. The provision made for reforming the battalion in a designated area after the game could have been more adequate. However, the cadets seemingly made no effort to reform anywhere . . . It is not likely that the privileges will be given back to us. However, if Major Seibert feels that the cadet corps conducts themselves in the manner in which they should, he may reconsider."[236]

Cadet Major Perrin McGee added his opinion to the controversy in another letter to the *Anvil*. "Men, I hope that you are satisfied with what you have done. You have cut your throats; consequently you will

---

[236] The *Kayemeye Anvil*, Vol. XII, No. 8, February 25, 1956.

not be receiving the normal privileges. You do not deserve a thing after the conduct which you have shown in the last two weeks, especially for the attitude at the basketball game on Wednesday night. When you take advantage of something which has been given to you, you are hurting yourself. As I have said before 'think' before you do something. You can do well if you want to do so . . ."[237]

Cadet Lt. Creed Smith tried to bury the hatchet by writing:

> When a basketball team loses a game, they usually try harder to win the next one. I sincerely believe that this is the way the students of the Kentucky Military Institute will react if given another chance. If Major Seibert will consider this I am sure that he will understand that there is no better time than the present to find out if he has been wrong in supporting the cadets' cause. If he does reconsider, I hope that each and every one of you will not let him down. There are always a few in each group who are relatively abject, but I am sure that the entire battalion has higher moral standards than was presented by this small minority of cadets.
>
> In conclusion, I would like to ask each one of you to make it known to Major Seibert that we do appreciate his efforts in trying to obtain more privileges for us. He has done more for us, and asked less in return, than anyone in our school.[238]

Major Seibert's stinging letter ended the public protest concerning the revoking of privileges. In May, Colonel Richmond alluded to the problem. The *Kentucadet* reported that the colonel was concerned: "Several things have happened this year because cadets have not reported incidents because they feel they would be squealing." He continued to say that there was a growing attitude of "you stick me" and "I'll stick you." He said that if he did not do anything else during the next year, he intended to teach more leadership ability and citizenship.[239] This statement reinforced the colonel's

---

[237] Letter to the Corps, Cadet Major McGee, the *Kayemeye Anvil*, Vol. XII, No. 8, February 25, 1956.

[238] Letter to the Editors, Creed Smith, the *Kayemeye Anvil*, Vol. XII, No. 8, February 25, 1956.

[239] Kayemeye *Anvil*, Vol. XII, No. 11, May 25, 1956, p. 6.

comments made in April concerning the attitude of the corps. He said the attitude of most cadets seemed to be improving. He "commented that the main reason for gripping is because we are actually trying to get out of doing something." He then emphasized the idea that a man's word is the most valuable thing he has. He stated his belief that the boys of today do not seem to be as basically truthful as the boys of ten years ago.[240]

The remainder of the term in Florida was relatively uneventful, until the last two nights spent in Venice. In an article in the *Sarasota Herald-Tribune* of May 5, 2002, entitled "KMI Carried City Through Lean Times," Fred Francis related that "when we'd run into the local guys, there could be trouble. The girls liked to see us. We all had Venice girlfriends, but the boys, that was trouble."[241] On March 27, 1956, the tension that existed between some of the local young men and the KMI cadets came to a head. According to Venice chief of police, John Shockey, he had received information that about two hundred teenage boys from Venice, Englewood, and Punta Gorda were coming to town to fight the cadets. Chief Shockey consulted with KMI officials, and it was decided that the cadets would be confined to their barracks for the night.

Chief Shockey issued an order that all teenagers had to be off the streets by 9:00 p.m. or they would be arrested. As word spread concerning the curfew, the boys began to disperse. The night ended without serious incident, but some of the boys vowed "We'll be back." The chief extended the curfew for a second night, and the KMI officials extended the confinement of the cadets to their rooms for another night. The incident ended the following day when the cadets boarded the KMI Special for the trip back to Kentucky.[242]

The major event for the ROTC detachment during the 1955-1956 school year was a bivouac held at Fort Knox. For three days, beginning on April 27, all of the cadets enrolled in the ROTC program participated in the field exercise. The bivouac was held over the weekend so that it would not interfere with normal classroom work and athletics.

On Saturday morning, the cadets, equipped with their rifles and full field packs, boarded buses for the trip to Fort Knox. Colonel Seibert remembered: "When the Corps fell out preparatory to boarding the buses

---

240   *Kayemeye Anvil*, Vol. XII, No. 10, April 24, 1956, p. 1.
241   *Sarasota Herald-Tribune*, May 5, 2002.
242   *St. Petersburg Times*, March 28, 1956.

for Ft. Knox, it was quite a spectacle. Some cadets looked as if they had been in the army for some time. These were mainly Boy Scouts. Others looked as if they had been hurriedly bundled in cast-off clothing. But all were enthusiastic. The Junior School cadets watched the buses depart wistfully."[243]

The purpose of the exercise was to train the cadets in small unit tactics and to give them a taste of life in the field. Blank ammunition had been acquired for the M1 rifles and the .30 machine guns. The school had purchased C-rations to feed the cadets during the exercise. The members of the Military Department instructed the cadets in the construction of field positions to include the digging of foxholes and the preparation of the C-rations. The use of artillery simulators and smoke kept the cadets on their toes. Throughout both nights, the cadets manning the machine guns kept most of the cadets awake and alert. The one drawback was an intermittent rain, which quickly turned the foxholes, roads, and the terrain into a muddy mess.

The cadets were divided into U.S. forces and aggressor forces for the purpose of the exercise. The U.S. forces were to find and fix the aggressors. Once this was accomplished, the U.S. forces took up a defensive position. The aggressor forces attacked the defenders and were repelled. After a night of probing actions by both forces, the U.S. forces attacked the aggressor's position. When the attack was concluded, the exercise was over. All that remained for the cadets was the march back to the buses. It had rained for several periods during the exercise, and the roads were muddy and everyone was wet and extremely tired. Major Seibert and the members of the military detachment moved up and down the slowly moving column, urging everyone to keep moving. The return to campus sent the entire battalion into hot showers and clean clothes. Once everyone was clean, the endless stories of the time spent at Fort Knox began.[244]

The May 25 issue of the *Kayemeye Anvil* brought up the only downside of the exercise:

> Although the Military Department was pleased with the spirit of the corps throughout the bivouac, the negligent

---

[243] Seibert, op. cit., p. 257.
[244] *Kayemeye Anvil*, Vol. XII, No. 10, April 24, 1956.

manner in which many of you treated your equipment branded the organization as "Green Horns" from the very first. If each person had brought his own equipment along, it stands to reason that the rifles wouldn't have been as maltreated or that the over government property wouldn't have been returned in as bad a shape. A lot of the corps has the mistaken idea that as long as equipment has "U.S." stamped on it, it can be treated without thinking. This idea was probably dispelled when you found out it wasn't to be returned in the sad mess it was brought back. At least the bivouac made a deep impression on several in the corps who immediately after returning joined the Army under the new Reserve plan.[245]

Despite the fact that the bivouac was deemed a success by the Military Department, the exercise was not repeated. The following year, a two-day field exercise was held on campus, and then the practice was dropped.[246]

As Major Seibert prepared to leave KMI for his next assignment as a student at the Ranger Course at Fort Benning, he decided not to attend the senior banquet. However, the NCOs in the Military Department, knowing what was going to happen, urged him to attend. The major was present when the president of the senior class announced that the *Saber* was dedicated to the major. He wrote, "I was surprised, honored and flattered. The copy presented to me was cherished until the footlocker in which I kept it was stolen. It was a good feeling to know that the cadets recognized what I had tried to do." Years after Colonel Seibert retired, some of the alumni learned that he had lost that *Saber*. One was found and shipped to him. When I interviewed the colonel nearly fifty years after that banquet, the *Saber* was in a prominent place on a bookshelf in his living room. Just as he had made a lasting impression on the corps of cadets, they apparently had made an equally lasting impression on him. [247]

In the months before Seibert left KMI, he raised the question of why the members of the Military Detachment had to pay the cost of their move to and from Florida. Because the orders moving the Detachment to

---

245 *Kayemeye Anvil*, Vol. XII, No. 11, May 25, 1956.
246 The *Kentucadet*, Vol. XXXII, No. 2, May, 1957, p. 4.
247 Seibert, op. cit., p. 258.

Florida specified that no expense would be incurred by the government, Seibert's request that mileage be paid was denied. When Seibert approached Colonel Richmond about the issue, the colonel denied the request stating that he was providing meals and rooms for the military personnel while they were in Florida.

The issue had not been resolved when Seibert departed. The new PMS&T, Major Ernest Poff, left the issue in the hands of Lt. Ray McClean for resolution. Lieutenant McClean had a heated meeting with Colonel Richmond. Apparently, the lieutenant lost his temper during the meeting which he described in a letter to Seibert: "But after a violent session with the Colonel, we were all transferred." The new school year started with an entirely new military department, except for Major Poff.[248]

Before leaving Lyndon, Major Seibert wrote a report in which he questioned the return that the army received for the money it expended on the ROTC program. Using numbers he received from the KMI Admissions Office and the alumni association, he felt the cost of the program was too high. His numbers indicated that only about 5 percent of the graduates went into college ROTC programs, a few went to the Service academies, and only about 3 percent served in the military. Although he admitted that the Junior ROTC program, according to Army Regulations, was to instill patriotism, he believed the cost was too high. In his thinking that the program should be a training ground for the military services, Seibert did not understand the driving educational philosophy of KMI.[249]

Writing in the 1914-1915 catalog, Colonel Fowler said, "An experience of six years as pupil and more than twenty-five years as teacher has convinced the Superintendent that the military discipline is the very best method of training boys for life . . . It not only gives the boy an upright and graceful carriage, but it teaches him obedience to rightful authority, cultivates the power of attention, and gives him promptness of decision and of action; and it is the only system of training that develops a boy's executive ability."[250]

In the 1932-1933 Catalog, Colonel Richmond stated clearly: "The object of the school is to prepare boys for colleges and universities, or to fit them for immediate entrance upon the duties and responsibilities of

---

[248] Seibert, op. cit., p. 258.

[249] Seibert, op. cit., p. 257.

[250] KMI Catalog, 1913-1914, p. 18.

life. Our plans have been shaped to meet this two fold need." He went on to say: "Military discipline is the best method of preparing a boy for life. It gives him an upright carriage, teaches him obedience to rightfully authority, cultivates is powers of attention, and develops promptness of decision and action. It brings out his executive ability as nothing else can do, for, having learned to obey, he is able to command."[251]

In a letter to the author's father, O. O. Pillans, director of admissions, described the courses open to prospective cadets in 1955 and the overall objective of the school. "K.M.I. has been a fully accredited college preparatory high school for over a century. We also have a junior school for boys in the seventh and eighth grades, a postgraduate school for high school graduates who seek further preparation for college, and a business school for those who plan to go directly into business." The purpose of the school was clearly stated: "We have a large faculty of boy specialists who give intelligent attention to the individual needs of each student. Our classes are small and our instruction is intensive and thorough. Our entire program of scholastic, military and physical training is planned to equip a boy for the duties and responsibilities he will be called upon to assume when he becomes a man."[252]

The 1952 Catalog summarized the school's purpose and the place the military system played in that purpose:

> Our primary purpose is not to train soldiers, however. It is to give thorough education, and naturally this includes military knowledge.
>
> Military training develops physique and graceful carriage. It establishes habits of system and order. The man who does his work without system and order, who has not been trained to do the right thing in the right way at the right time, will always labor at a disadvantage, especially when brought into competition with others so trained.
>
> Placing cadets in command of companies and smaller units, and holding them strictly responsible for the efficient and impartial performance of duty, gives executive training that has

---

[251] KMI Catalog, 1932-1933, pp. 33 and 38.
[252] O. O. Pillans to Dr. T. R. Young, February 10, 1955.

no equivalent in the non-military school. Responsiveness to duty, service to associates and promotion of common interests become second nature.[253]

The military training at KMI was not intended to produce soldiers; it was, as stated by Major Alex Hodgin in 1971: "dispelling a myth that military schools are prep schools for institutions like West Point and military careers . . . the central emphasis at K.M.I. is on the academic rather than the military training that taught them orderliness and discipline."[254]

In the spring of 1957, ten members of the KMI choir were selected to be a part of the Kentucky All-state Chorus, which was composed of approximately 350 students selected from high school glee clubs and choirs from across the state. After two days of practice in April, the chorus performed at the Kentucky Education Association Convention in Lexington. The participation of a select number of choir members at the convention was an annual affair for a number of years.[255]

On October 2, 1957, about eighty-five members of the cadet corps participated in the premier of the movie Raintree County at the Brown Theater in downtown Louisville. The cadet officers stood at attention on either side of the platform where the celebrities in attendance were introduced. The remaining cadets formed

Members of the Cadet Choir—Claibourne

on either side of the path between the theater and the Brown Hotel. The cadets who did not attend the premier were envious of those who did attend—not only did they spend the evening in Louisville, but they had also seen Elizabeth Taylor.[256]

---

253 KMI Catalog, 1952, p. 88.
254 *L&N Magazine*, February, 1971, p. 14.
255 *Kayemeye Anvil*, Vol. XIII, No. 6, March 15, 1957.
256 *Kayemeye Anvil*, Vol. XIV, No. 1, October 26, 1957, p. 3.

A few days after the premier, the Asian flu epidemic that was sweeping the country struck KMI. The outbreak started slowly, but very quickly, Ms. Evelyn "Maw" Fowler and her small ten-bed infirmary was overwhelmed. At first, the cadets who could not get into the infirmary were sent to their rooms, but this quickly proved to be completely impractical. The Military Department obtained army cots, probably from the Kentucky National Guard or Fort Knox, and turned the gym into a makeshift hospital. Those cadets who were sick in the barracks were moved to the gym, and newly stricken cadets quickly joined them. It was not surprising that the flu spread so rapidly through the student body. Living in such close quarters, it was surprising that anyone escaped the disease. Cadets who avoided contracting the flu continued to attend class until no instructors remained to teach the classes. At its peak, there were no more than three tables of cadets eating in the dining room. For perhaps the first time in the school's history, there was no vespers service on October 20 because the gym was full of cots and sick cadets. The flu quickly moved through the school, and by Thursday, enough cadets had recovered sufficiently to hold a pep rally before the football game with Culver. Unlike the 1918 Spanish flu epidemic when one cadet died, KMI fared well during the flu outbreak. More than seventy thousand people in the United States died during the flu epidemic.

Cadets at the Premier of Raintree County—Young

On Wednesday night, November 26, 1958, every cadet was crowded around a television set in the barracks. Although Thanksgiving was the next day, no one was thinking about a day off, visits by parents, and a big turkey dinner. Everyone was waiting for Ralph Edwards and *This Is Your Life* to begin. The honored guest was to be Jim Backus, a former KMI cadet. One of the guests scheduled to surprise Backus was Colonel Richmond. The two men had not seen each other in twenty-eight years, and everyone was eager to see what the two had to say to each other. It was a little anticlimactic. The meeting was cordial, but little was said about Backus's time at KMI. Most of the cadets were disappointed that Colonel Richmond had no good stories to tell about Cadet Backus. However, it would have been completely out of character for the colonel to bring up any misconduct on the part of Cadet Backus in front of a national television audience.

Ralph Edwards, Colonel Richmond, and Jim Backus—Young

Chapter IX

THE FINAL YEARS

One thing that should never be forgotten throughout most of its history, KMI was a school for boys. Despite the military discipline and strict rules, the saying that "boys will be boys" was valid at KMI. There were always some cadets who were willing to push the rules to their limit, and frequently beyond. Some of the stunts and pranks became a part of the folklore of the school, and others simply were repeated with each new group of cadets. The cadets were well aware of the punishments for violating the rules and accepted the consequences of their actions. The comments concerning Major Byars in 1921 would have applied throughout most of the school's history. "He realizes that we must raise cain occasionally and altho he never hesitates to give us the punishment the Blue Book prescribes, we know that he does not hold an occasional infraction of the rules against us."[257]

A Parting Message—Brinker

Some pranks had possible far reaching effects. The painting of the sign on the gym roof the night before commencement in 1959 was one of those events. The author spent about thirty minutes, it

---

[257] *Saber*, 1921.

seemed like several hours, at attention in front of Colonel Hodgin's desk at 5:30 a.m. Also present was Colonel Richmond and Major Bart Williams, and the questions of who the culprit might be were nonstop. Fortunately, I had attended the commencement dance and had absolutely no idea who had painted the sign. At one point, Colonel Richmond implied that commencement exercises might be delayed until the guilty party was identified. That was probably a hollow threat since the number of guests coming to the ceremony made a delay or cancellation unlikely. It would be fifty years before I learned the name of the painter, who should forever remain a legend.

At some point, a cadet or two thought that flushing an M-80 or a .30 caliber blank with a fuse attached down a toilet was a good idea. The end result was a job for the school's maintenance crew. No cadets were injured, and it is fortunate that the devices never cleared the toilets. An explosion in the sewage pipes might have caused much more damage.

Perhaps the most daring prank was to slip into the guardhouse late at night and play bugle calls or a rock and roll record over the public address system. The problem was not in getting to the guardhouse; it was starting the record and getting away without being seen. Occasionally, the offender would be caught, but it seemed that someone was willing to try it at least once a year. A similar stunt was activating the sound system located in the gym. Designed to play music through

OOPS! Something Went Slightly Wrong—Tullis

speakers mounted on the gym roof, it could play loud enough to wake up most of the cadet corps.

Over the years, several low-powered radio stations, appropriately known as WKMI, were clandestinely operated by the cadets. The stations used radio-sending sets assembled by the cadets and did not send a signal much beyond the main barracks area. One of the stations used a tape recorder to play music continuously for several hours without interruption. The operation of the stations probably violated FCC regulations, but there was little or no effort by the school to shut down the stations. It is certain that a few members of the faculty knew who was operating the stations, but they decided to look the other way.

Wall climbing in the San Marco has been mentioned, but the cadets explored other areas of the campus. The attics of the Venice Hotel and Ormsby Hall attracted the attention of numerous cadets. One of the more unusual sites visited was under B Barracks. There was no basement, and only a low crawl space filled with pipes, wires, and cobwebs. The problem with exploring under the barracks was it required cutting a hole in the floor to gain access to the space.

One of the things that the Old Boys made certain that the New Boys knew about was the Ormsby family treasure. The story was told that during the Civil War, the slaves on the Ormsby plantation had taken all of the family silver and other valuables and buried them on the plantation when they heard that the Yankees were coming. Since only the few slaves who had buried the treasure knew its actual location and they were sold down

Exploring Under B Barracks—Tullis

the river, the treasure was never recovered. It is difficult to estimate how much of the KMI campus was dug up over the years by cadets looking for the treasure. Apparently, the Ormsby treasure legend extended well beyond the boundaries of the campus. Betty Kay Hammock Utley, who lived with her parents on the Lyndon campus, remembers local Blacks singing and digging in the area of the lake in search of the Ormsby gold and silver.[258]

According to the Blue Book, all barracks rooms were to be properly ventilated at all times. After taps, the windows were to be open, regardless of the outside temperature. This rule resulted in one of the duties of the Rats and was also the source of tricks played on the unsuspecting cadet.

[258] Conversation between Betty Kay Hammock Utley and the author, January 25, 2013.

Each morning, before the heat was turned on in the barracks, one of the New Boys on each stoop was responsible for closing all of the windows on the floor. It was important for his continued health that he not wake up any of the sleeping Old Men when he closed their windows. There were some risks involved in the duty, trip wires were set, wastebaskets filled with water where placed over the doors, and other traps were set for the unsuspecting cadet.

Other pranks, which were more irritating than dangerous, included such things as the following: short sheeting beds, so the cadet had to remake the bed in the dark; filling a bed with shaving cream; smearing limburger cheese on the back of a radiator when the heat was off, a trick that would quickly empty a room when the heat came on; removing springs from a bed so it would collapse when the cadet climbed in; fire crackers and cherry bombs exploding during the night; bowling balls and shot being rolled down the hall late at night; to name only a few. In addition, there were such things as aerosol shaving cream fights, water fights, and general rough housing.

Each autumn, a few cadets could be found bringing gallon jugs of apple cider, raisins, and packages of yeast onto campus. Other cadets tried their hand at fermenting grape juice in an effort to produce homemade wine. After the ingredients were combined, the jugs were concealed in a warm dark place for several weeks. If the jugs were not found and confiscated by faculty members or moved by other cadets, the brew master would finally strain the mixture, and he and a few friends would consume the mixture. Whether the mixture had much alcoholic content is open to speculation, but the cadets thought it did, and that was all that mattered to them. One unintended consequence of the process was when the brewer forgot to punch holes in the lid of the glass jug and the container broke or, in some cases, exploded. If the jug was hidden in a room, the mess and smell was certain to draw much unwanted attention and a tour of duty on the beat.

Cadets had their own methods of dealing with cadets who broke

That's About Right!—Young

rules. In many cases, a forceful talking to by an upperclassman was sufficient to make a cadet see the error of his ways. If that was not effective, the "Silent Treatment" was very effective in making a cadet aware that he needed to change his behavior. Not to be talked to by anyone for several days usually prompted the offender to alter his behavior. On some occasions, but only for serious offensives such as stealing, the cadet might be subjected to some physical punishment, usually by being placed in the "Bull Ring." In rare instances, when a cadet committed a particularly serious offense, he would be the subject of a "Blanket Party." The offending cadet would be accosted after he was in bed and taps had sounded. He would have a blanket thrown over his head, and he would be pummeled with fists by several cadets. The cadet had no idea who had rendered the beating, and he bore few marks to indicate that he had been attacked. It would have been unlikely that the cadet would fail to heed the warning such a punishment conveyed.

When there were serious difference between cadets, fights might occur, usually where they would not be observed by the faculty. At various times during the school's history, there were provisions for faculty members to supervise fights between individual cadets. The faculty member was to see that the fight was fair and that no one was seriously injured. Generally, serious differences between cadets were resolved without resorting to physical violence. Mutual friends would step in to negotiate a settlement, or the cadets would just avoid each other.[259]

One particular punishment administered to cadets who neglected their personal hygiene was the broom bath. Cadets were expected to take at least three showers a week, but some seemed to have an aversion to warm water and soap. After the cadet was warned about his hygiene problem and he refused to correct the problem, he was treated to a bath. He would be taken to the showers, stripped of his clothes, and thrown into the hot shower. He was then washed with brooms and powdered bathroom cleaner by other cadets. Only a few cadets ever wanted to repeat the experience. One cadet receiving the bath usually persuaded other cadets who might have neglected their hygiene that they did not want to receive the same punishment.

---

[259]   Undated Blue Book, Article 63, p. 11.

Raleigh Sallee, a 1960 graduate, asserted that "most K.M.I. cadets were there at the insistence of their parents. Some were allowed to share in varying degrees in this decision. Some seriously didn't want to be there but were required to remain. Naturally and understandably, many cadets were not fully committed to pursuing KMI ideals. Acceptance and pursuit of ideals varied greatly."[260] It is impossible to know how many students wanted to attend KMI and how many were sent and forced to remain in school by their parents.

Each year, a few students left school, some with their parents' permission but others simply went Absent Without Leave (AWOL). Some of those who went AWOL were brought back by their parents; others never returned. Other cadets tried to beat the system but found themselves unable to prevail against the system. In many cases, those cadets who refused to conform to the discipline imposed on the cadets found themselves as permanent fixtures on the beat.

In the nineteenth century, cadets had been awarded demerits for infractions of rules and regulations. At some point in the twentieth century, the policy of awarding cadets a merit for each day they received no demerits was started. The Blue Book stated that "demerits are not punishment, but a means of rating cadets in conduct. They will be awarded for every report which is not marked satisfactory or removed."[261] Each merit a cadet received would cancel two demerits.

In addition to demerits, there were additional penalties "which a cadet shall be liable, in addition to the number of demerits awarded for the offense are as follows: Confinement to restricted limits, penalty tours, reprimand, reduction of officers and non-commissioned officers, dismissal and expulsion." When a cadet did not have sufficient merits to

Walking the Beat—Brinker

260 http://www.kmialumni.org/alumni/roster_main.html.
261 Undated Blue Book, Article 46.

cancel his demerits, he would be required to walk penalty tours which were "served every afternoon after drill and on Mondays. Each tour will be fifty minutes' marching, with ten minutes' rest between consecutive tours."[262]

Confinement consisted of two different forms: to "On Bounds" or "Yard Limits" in Kentucky and to his room. A cadet confined to his room could only leave for classes, drill, and meals. All other times during the day, he had to be in his room. He could only leave with permission of the officer of the day to go to the hospital, the bathroom, or to take a shower. Cadets "On Bounds" or "Yard Limits" in Kentucky were restricted to the area of the barracks, tennis courts, athletic field, and academic buildings. In Florida, the cadet was restricted to the barracks, tennis court, basketball court, and the area between the San Marco and the Venice. The cadet was not permitted to cross the street in front of the San Marco or visit any of the stores in Venice.

Cadets who had to work off demerits or were confined lost their free time after drill during the week and on Saturday or Monday. During much of the twentieth century, classes were held Tuesday through Saturday with Monday off. At other times, classes were held Monday through Friday, with Saturday off. For instance, in 1958, the school holiday was on Saturday until Christmas vacation, after which the holiday was on Monday for the remainder of the year.

School administrators tried to retain students and worked to correct discipline problems without expelling students. In 1956, for example, two cadets were expelled: one for willful and continual defiance of school rules and policies and the other for continual disobedience of school rules after having been placed on probation for removing wire from the loud speakers, for skipping formations and study hall, and for being absent without leave. The fact that both cadets were cited for "continual" defiance and disobedience indicates that the students had been given ample opportunity to modify their conduct and conform to school rules and policies before being expelled.

In May 1960, the *Kentucadet* republished an article it had originally published in May 1958. The article emphasized the "Role of the Private Military School in America" and opened with a statement that "public

---

[262] Undated Blue Book, Articles 119 and 121.

high schools are lagging far behind private secondary schools in leadership production." Citing a report by *Who's Who in America*, the conclusion was drawn that "the private schools in America are doing a splendid job in turning out leaders in all walks of life."

The administrators at the Kentucky Military Institute are proud to have a part in the job the private schools in America are doing. With us the military is not the ultimate goal. College preparation occupies the spotlight. However, the military system, in our opinion, offers the most efficient means of operating a college preparatory school. We feel that the marriage of the military system to the college preparatory curriculum produces an informed, poised, and physically developed boy. We are proud of our finished product.[263]

Cadets in Class—Venice

In an appeal to alumni and patrons of the school, the *Kentucadet* published a notice on the school's admissions policy in 1957. Because of the projected increase in applications to colleges and universities, it was predicted that entrance requirements would be increased. The increased requirements would have a significant impact on KMI when accepting new cadets. Since at least 90 percent of the graduates went on to college, the school would have to be more selective in admitting new students. KMI required that:

> Each applicant fill out an admission blank giving full details concerning himself. 1. Two character references are required; blanks are sent to the references furnished us. 2. We require a transcript of grades and, most important, a record

---

[263]   The *Kentucadet*, Vol. XXXV, No. 2, May 1960, p. 12 and The *Kentucadet*, Vol. XXXIII, No. 2, May 1958, p. 12.

of standardized test scores, including a scholastic aptitude test. In the absence of these test scores, we will administer or send to the home town to be administered, test of our own. 3. A personal interview is always obtained if possible. On the basis of these facts, the school is then able to make judgment as to admission.

It is interesting that the *Kentucadet* published the same appeal in 1963.[264]

In an effort to give the cadets experience in exercising responsibility, the daily activities of the school were controlled by the members of the guard detail. The detail worked under the supervision of a faculty member, the officer in charge, and followed a schedule drawn up by the administration, but the cadet officer of the day was responsible for seeing that the day went according to schedule. The members of the guard detail wore white shirts and the garrison cap with white cover to distinguish them from the rest of the cadets. Those cadets who were authorized also wore their Sam Browne belts. For much of the twentieth century, the guard detail consisted of a cadet officer or senior noncommissioned officer, a sergeant, a corporal, and a private. Early in the period, there was a commander of the guard, who ranked below the officer of the day, and no corporal of the guard. "The Officer of the Day is required to report all irregularities, neglects, breaches of discipline, or other acts inconsistent with the provisions of these regulations [the Blue Book] or with the soldiery or moral character of cadets which may come to his notice."[265] Before the installation of the public address system, a bugler was a member of the detail. The detail was responsible for playing the bugle calls that woke

"They Stuck Me for That?"—Young

---

[264] The *Kentucadet*, Vol. XXXII, No. 3, May 1957, p. 12 and the *Kentucadet*, Vol. XXXVII, No. 3, May 1963, p. 15.

[265] Undated Blue Book, Article 72, Paragraph J, p. 13.

the cadets, called them to meals, classes, drill, and their quarters and finally put them to bed. The members of the detail collected attendance reports for classes, formations, and calls to quarters. When a cadet was absent, the detail determined whether or not his absence was authorized and reported him if he did not have permission to miss class or a formation.

From the glass-enclosed guardhouse, the detail observed the activities in the central campus area. Room inspections were made during class periods to make sure that cadets were not congregating when they should have been studying. During the afternoon recreation period, rooms were checked to make sure that no cadets were in their rooms when they should have been outside. During evening study hall, the detail watched the porches of A and B Barracks to make sure that cadets remained in their rooms. They also began the process of organizing the various "Stick Sheets" that had been turned in during the day so that the report sheets could be typed and posted the next day. After taps, one or two members of the detail were released, but the officer of the day and the sergeant of the guard usually remained on duty until dismissed by the officer in charge. The next morning, after reveille, the guard detail was relieved by a new detail.

"But My Shoes Were Shined!"—Young

Although the guard detail was responsible for a number of activities, the experience gained by the cadets by serving in the various positions on the detail over the years gave the cadets the necessary experience to carry out their duties. Although the officer of the day supervised the guard detail and had specific duties, "He shall have general supervision of the routine during his tour of duty, shall direct the Cadet Officer of the Day in the performance of his duties, shall make such inspections of quarters and buildings as the President or Commandant may direct or as in his judgment may seem necessary, shall take prompt measures to check all irregularities, abuses, or violations of regulations or order that may come to his knowledge and shall consider himself responsible for the proper carrying out of the daily routine."[266] In most cases, the officer in charge allowed the detail to perform its duties with a minimum of interference. Guard duty was designed to teach the cadets how to perform their duties, learn from their mistakes, and assume the responsibilities of their position.

It is interesting to note that the duties of the private of the guard changed over the years. In an early Blue Book, it was specified that:

> The Private of the Guard shall be dressed at all times, when on duty, in blouse, white shirt, black tie, grey trousers and cap. He will remain in the hall or main office of Ormsby Hall, except when sent on duty elsewhere. He will meet all visitors and show them into the living rooms. The Private of the Guard will be relieved from duty at Taps.[267]

In a later edition of the Blue Book, the duties of the private of the guard were changed and limited:

> The Private of the Guard will remain in the Guard Room except when sent on duty elsewhere. He will show all visitors into the reception rooms. The Private of the Guard is responsible for the police of the Guard Room. Under no circumstances shall the Private of the Guard enter reports, handle permits, report cadets on or off or have anything to do with the duties of the Officer of the Day or the commander of the Guard. The Private of the Guard will be relieved from duty at Taps."[268]

During the 1960s, a program was started to update many of the facilities on the Lyndon campus. The Edison Science Building, A and B Barracks as well as Gregg Hall had all been state-of-the-art facilities when they were constructed. However, time, as well as the normal wear and tear of forty to fifty years of continuous use, had taken their toll on the buildings.

In 1960, a new classroom building was constructed behind A Barracks. Four years later, a second classroom building was constructed adjacent to

---

[266] Undated Blue Book, Article 79, pp. 16-17.
[267] Undated Blue Book, Article 76, p. 13.
[268] Undated Blue Book, Article 84, p. 19.

the first building. Each of the buildings contained eight modern classrooms. Both of the new buildings were of concrete construction with reinforced concrete foundation. The rooms had rubber tile floors and acoustical ceilings, and each room had thermostatically controlled gas heating. The new rooms had fluorescent lights, new blackboards, and bulletin boards as well as new furniture. Most of the work on the new buildings was done by KMI's maintenance crew. To make room for the second building, the QM building was moved and renovated. With the exception of the laboratory facilities, the chemistry and biology laboratories had also been updated, and the military classrooms and the new buildings were the academic center of the school.[269]

Also improved in 1964 was the school library. The second floor of the Edison Science Building was extensively remodeled to make room for the new facility. The numerous partitions that had divided the area into six classrooms were removed. New shelving, periodical racks, and study desks with chairs were installed. The new area would accommodate about forty students at a time for study. The library was completely carpeted to reduce the amount of noise. The school was one of three in Jefferson County experimenting with carpet to reduce the sound in school rooms. The new library was to begin a reference reserve system, whereby books could be placed in a special area if it was needed for a particular class. The additional space in the new library meant that a large number of newspapers and magazines needed for reports, and term papers could be retained.[270]

The New Library—Reichspfarr

To provide improved living areas for the faculty, several improvements were made in 1964. Three rooms in A Barracks, 100, 200, and 300, were remodeled to provide quarters for bachelor faculty members. The

---

[269] The *Adjutant's Call*, Vol. XX, No. 1, October 17, 1964.
[270] The *Adjutant's Call*, Vol. XX, No. 1, October 17, 1964.

most extensive work required was the addition of bath facilities. With the remodeling of these rooms, at least one member of the faculty was living on each floor of the barracks throughout the school. To accommodate the married faculty members living in Gregg Hall, an addition added three rooms to the building. The addition meant that each married faculty member had a three-room apartment with kitchen facilities. The faculty apartments were also redecorated as a part of the expansion.[271]

In the fall of 1964, Dr. Simpson and family returned to KMI after a two-year leave of absence. He had taken the leave to work on his PhD degree in administration and management at the University of Kentucky. He assumed the duties of assistant to the president and coordinator of instruction for the 1964-65 school year. He also resumed his duties as the head basketball coach.[272]

In September 1966, the cadets returned to find that major renovations had been made to B Barracks. The first floor of the barracks had new tile floors, fluorescent lights, and new sinks in every room. In addition, new desks, closets, drawers, and cabinets had been placed in the newly remodeled rooms. New wiring, as well as new plumbing and heating pipes, had been added to the entire building. Dr. Simpson told the cadets that the remodeling was an experiment. If the cadets took care of the new rooms, a floor would be renovated each year. In an effort to be fair, straws were drawn and D Company was the first group of cadets to be able to use the new rooms. The *Adjutant's Call* for November 1966 reported that there were many favorable comments about the new rooms during homecoming weekend.[273]

In addition to the improvements being made by the school, alumni and friends of the school were making gifts to improve the physical plant. The Class of '65 gave an electronic football scoreboard to the school. The father of a former cadet, Mark Forrester, Class of '66, gave the school a new sprinkling system for the football field. The *Adjutant's Call* of October 1966 anticipated the construction of a new chapel by the alumni association as soon as funds were available. It was noted in the article that the land had already been deeded to the association.

---

[271] The *Kentucadet*, October 1964, p. 3.
[272] William T. Simpson to the author, January 22, 2013.
[273] The *Adjutant's Call*, Vol. XXII, No. 1, October, 1966.

A physical training program was started in the fall of 1964. The program consisted of two parts: a series of exercises after each period of drill and four tests to be given during the year. The tests were to consist of pull-ups, push-ups, squat thrusts, sit-ups, and a three-hundred-yard run. The first test, held September 26, found Cadet George Ward compiling a score of 482 points out of a possible 500. The program of exercises was to be increased by adding one repetition of each exercise each week. The Military Department was highly satisfied with the results of the first test and expected the scores to improve. The department felt that the program would not only build up the cadets but also develop teamwork and unit effort.[274] Cadets from a decade earlier might wonder what had happened to the physical training program that had been conducted under the watchful eye of Major Seibert. They would remember double timing to the front gate and sit-ups and push-ups at selected afternoon sessions, all intended to improve the physical well-being of the cadets.

One of the most important events of any year was the Annual Government Inspection. Beginning in 1914, KMI carried the designation by the War Department as an Honor School. Initially, KMI was placed in Class M of the military schools under the supervision of the government. The schools in this class were "Essentially military institutions where the curriculum is not sufficiently advanced to carry with it a degree, or where the average age on graduation is less then twenty-one years."[275] Initially, no more than ten schools were awarded the Honor School rating.

Standing Inspection—Claibourne

Initially, the government inspections had been held several times a year, but by the 1950s, only one inspection was held each year. At the designated time, a team of Regular Army officers would descend on the

---

274   The *Adjutant's Call*, Vol. XX, No. 1, October 17, 1964.
275   KMI Catalog, 1914-1915, pp. 19-20.

school for the annual inspection. Occasionally, the inspection was held late in the Florida term, but usually it was held after the school had returned to Kentucky. The officers inspected all aspects of the military training that the cadets received. The team members attended military classes, and a question and answer session was held at the end of each class. Student rooms were inspected by a member of the school's military department and the inspecting officers. The final event of the inspection was a review of the corps and then an inspection of the ranks. The inspectors carefully watched the performance of the cadets during the drill and inspected the appearance and knowledge of the cadets during the inspection of the cadets in formation.[276]

Over the years, the weeks leading up to the government inspection were extremely busy. Cadets cleaned and painted their rooms; they washed windows and waxed floors and furniture; they had their hair cut to prescribed length; uniforms were inspected and repaired; and the intensity of afternoon drills increased dramatically. The school's maintenance people worked to repair any of the school's facilities. While some of the cadets viewed all of their painting, washing, and waxing as a cheap way to maintain the barracks rooms, all of the preparations paid dividends. For a number of years, prizes were awarded to the cadets who had the neatest room on their stoop. At various times, the prizes consisted of a cash award; and at other times, when the inspection was held before the school left Florida, an extra day of vacation leave was granted. For those cadets who believed that their rooms were spotless, there were a few cadets who could inspect a room and find problems. The inspection, known as a White Gloves Inspection, might find dust on the inside of the coiled springs of bunk beds or on light bulbs and quickly bring the neatest room occupants back to reality.

The government inspection criteria were stiffened in 1957, when the number of schools that would be designated as Honor Schools was reduced. KMI would earn the Honor School rating every year from 1914 until it lost the designation in 1967. The school, through a concerted effort on the part of the cadets, regained the rating in 1968 and retained it until the school closed in 1971.[277]

---

[276] The *Kayemeye Anvil*, Vol. XII, No. 10, April 24, 1956, p. 1.

[277] Email from Leon Hirsh to the author, February 26, 2013.

One benefit of achieving the Honor School rating was that the school could nominate candidates to compete for appointments to West Point. The nominated students took competitive exams along with the candidates from the other Honor Schools. In 1955, two cadets, Samuel Gin and Keith Rhea, won appointments to West Point. The previous year, one cadet had won appointment to West Point and another to Annapolis.[278]

In an environment that fostered competition among the cadets, KMI instituted a number of awards to recognize outstanding achievements. "One innate drive in every person is to achieve in some activity. Along with this is the inner satisfaction that is gained when public recognition is made of this achievement." The awards were divided into special awards, academic, military, and athletic honors.[279]

The highest award that the faculty could bestow on a cadet was selection of the seniors to be inducted into the Legion of Honor. The faculty selection committee collected information throughout the school year on a nominee's activities. Information was collected from the military department, the commandant's office, the headmaster, instructors, coaches, and the sponsors of various clubs. The information collected was given to the members of the faculty to help them make their decision. The cadets who received the votes of a majority of the faculty were the new members of the legion. No more than 10 percent of the senior class could be selected for the reward.[280]

Colonel Richmond Recognizes New Members of the Legion of Honor—Claibourne

Competition for the valedictorian award was often fierce among the seniors. Everyone in the corps knew who the contenders for the award were because the class standings were posted along with grade averages. The award was given to the individual in the senior class with the

---

[278] The *Kentucadet: Alumni Journal*, Vol. XXX, No. 4, May 1955, p. 3.
[279] *Cadet Honors*, Kentucky Military Institute, 1956.
[280] The *Kayemeye Anvil*, Vol. XII, No. 8, February 25, 1956.

highest scholastic average. The average was figured only on the class work done during the cadet's senior year. In 1956, the editors of the *Kayemeye Anvil* ask if the basis for the valedictorian award might be changed to a more impartial basis. The problem with basing the award on only work done the senior year was that a student might take a number of snap courses in which he would receive higher grades than his overall work might merit. However, the editors recognized that basing the award on the entire high school record would be unfair to a cadet who had attended KMI for four years if he was in competition with someone who had attended another school with less stringent standards and then transferred to KMI. The editors offered no solution to the problem, and the existing process remained in place.[281]

There were a number of competitions that were based on military performance: best drilled cadet, best drilled squad, best drilled platoon, neatest cadet, and neatest room. All of these various competitions attracted the attention of many of the cadets throughout the year. The most important competition was for the Alumni Association Military Trophy awarded to the Best Company. The importance of the Best Company competition was perhaps best summed up by Major Seibert. "Even at this age, personal ambitions and animosities were subordinated to unit pride; every cadet wanted his Company to be named 'Best Company' . . . The cadets were on edge. Finally I pronounced A Company the 'Best Company.' Pandemonium broke loose! A Company cadets jumped and screamed, losing control of themselves. The other companies, dejected, turned away in disappointment. It meant a great deal to these young men that they could wear a patch on their sleeves which said 'Best Company.'"[282] On only one point was the major mistaken, cadets did not wear a Best Company patch, they wore a yellow citation cord on their uniform for the remainder of their time at KMI. The Best Squad wore the patch on their uniform that the major mentioned.

The Best Company competition was a year-long affair that involved virtually all aspects of the cadets' life. There were three major drill competitions during the year in which the companies competed against each other. In addition, the scores from the best drilled platoon, best

[281] The *Kayemeye Anvil*, Vol. XII, No. 11, May 25, 1956.
[282] Seibert, op. cit., pp. 246-247.

drilled squad, best drilled cadet, neatest cadet, and neatest room competitions were counted toward the final score. In addition, the academic performance of the cadets in each company was factored into the final score. Also included in the final score were the results of the year's intramural competition between the companies.

Sports and physical activities were always an important part of the cadet's life. In the early years, there was a period of calisthenics early in the morning. The first mention of football was in 1887, when seventeen cadets made up the team. Some of the first improvements made after the move to Lyndon were sports facilities. In 1898, a gymnasium was constructed. In 1900, a bicycle and running track were constructed as well as baseball and football fields and several tennis courts. The organized teams that existed at the turn of the century were baseball, football, track, and tennis. Undoubtedly, those cadets who did not participate in organized sports took part in intramurals or individual sports activities.[283]

Throughout the twentieth century, KMI teams would compete in a number of organized sports. For those cadets interested in football and basketball, there were varsity and junior varsity teams; and in the case of football, there was another team for the younger and smaller cadets. Other sports such as tennis, golf, track, baseball, cross country, soccer, and swimming, there was only a varsity team. Over the years, various teams had very good seasons, such as the 1947 football team and the three-year winning streak of the basketball team from 1946 to 1948. In 1956, the golf team won the state meet; the basketball team was a finalist in the Florida regional tournament; the swimming team was fourth in the state meet; and the baseball team

State Champions—L to R, Dave Pedley, Ronnie Howard, Colonel Richmond, George Stigger, and Dick Canon—*Saber*

---

[283] Simpson, op. cit., pp. 96 and 111.

was a finalist in the district tournament. In both 1955 and 1956, Cadet George Stigger won the high school state golf championship.[284]

For those cadets who did not participate in the organized sports program, there was an extensive intramural program. Each of the companies entered teams in such sports as touch football, basketball, tennis, swimming, and track competitions. The intramurals were important in the competition for the Best Company award. The cadets took the games seriously, and they were usually very spirited and highly competitive. One cadet stated that the only difference between playing varsity and intramural football was "We didn't wear pads." In addition to the organized and intramural programs, there were occasional matches between cadets and members of the faculty and military department that always drew large and enthusiastic crowds. Surprisingly, many of the cadets supported the faculty teams. The most highly competitive contests were between the cadets and the members of the military department.

On March 29, 1966, Dr. Simpson delivered an address to the members of the Association of Military Colleges and Schools entitled "The Next Fifty Years." The purpose of the address was to examine trends in education which would provide information to help plan for what might happen in the next fifty years. Simpson predicted the demise of the proprietary school in the coming years. He noted that in the last few years, there had been a significant reorganization of military schools into various nonprofit forms. The reorganization had been done to take advantage of new tax benefits and various forms of increased federal aid. It was his opinion that the proprietary schools could not compete with the reorganized schools.

The changes taking place in the American family, the move toward urbanization, away from the era of the small town and farm, offered military boarding schools the opportunity to fill an obvious void. The family's role in educating and molding its children was diminishing. Simpson went on to assert that "the military boarding school should prosper during the next fifty years for it can meet the demands of the times. The boarding school can fulfill the role of the family surrogate. The military system of organization can provide the involvement necessary to developing an adequate self-image."

---

[284] Cadet Honors, Kentucky Military Institute, 1956. The Kentucky Country Day website lists many of the KMI athletic achievements.

Simpson then touched on Major Seibert's question concerning the value the government received in return for the money spent on the ROTC programs. The Department of Defense measured the ROTC programs by the number of officers produced. Simpson admitted that the schools were lacking in that respect. In view of the changing attitude toward the military that was developing in the 1960s, he believed that the military schools had a public relations role to play. It was necessary to educate people to respect and understand the need for military forces. He concluded that, "the development of patriotism, character, and citizenship are goals of the R.O.T.C. program. I am not convinced the government money is less well spent when the R.O.T.C. program develops an outstanding civilian leader who has respect for the military than it is when it develops a military leader."

Simpson concluded his presentation with a statement and a question: "I believe the broader view of the program is imminent. The immediate question is, can you and I as school administrators have the patience to wait for it?"[285]

In an article published in *Virginia Living* in 2005, Tom Prunier recounted the demise of military high schools that Simpson had discussed. At one time, the state of Virginia had almost fifty military high schools. In 2005, there were only seven still in operation. The schools had once advertised extensively, and their recruiting ads could be found beside KMI's in numerous magazines such as *National Geographic* and *Boy's Life*. Prunier said that the 1960s were a time of high attrition for military schools. "More than two-thirds of America's military high schools closed due to declining enrollment, cuts in federal subsidies and change in attitudes toward the military, largely because of Vietnam."[286]

Both Colonel Richmond and Lieutenant Colonel Hodgin relinquished their positions at KMI in 1965 after forty years of service. Through the efforts of these two men, KMI had been resurrected in 1925 and built into what was arguably the finest military preparatory school in the United States. They were replaced by Dr. William T. Simpson as president and Major Charles "Alex" A. Hodgin as commandant. Dr. Simpson was

---

[285] William T. Simpson, "The Next Fifty Years," An Address to the Association of Military Colleges and Schools, March 29, 1966.

[286] Tom Prunier, "Virginia's Military School Tradition," *Virginia Living*, February, 2005, p. 120.

Colonel Richmond's son-in-law, having married his daughter Diane Dixon Richmond. Major Hodgin was the son of Lt. Col. C. E. Hodgin and a 1949 graduate of KMI. Major Hodgin was one of the few individuals who had grown up on the KMI campus, attended and graduated from the school, and then returned to be a teacher and administrator.

In the span of only eight months, KMI lost three of the men who had come from Greenbriar Military School and built KMI into one of the premier preparatory schools in the nation. On June 8, 1968, Colonel Sam Marshall died at his farm in West Virginia when a tractor he was driving rolled over on him. On December 23, 1968, Colonel Richmond died in Venice Florida; although retired, the Colonel was in Venice supervising the preparations for the arrival of the cadet corps for the winter term. On January 19, 1969, Colonel Groseclose died in the hospital in Venice. Although all three men were retired, they had continued participating in various KMI activities. Colonel C. E. Hodgin, the fourth member of the Greenbriar Four, would remain active in various KMI events until the school closed. In March of 1988, the KMI Educational Foundation presented the colonel with the Spirit of Excellence award. The colonel continued to participate in various alumni activities until his death in 1997.

One of the stabilizing influences at KMI during the Richmond years was the long tenure of its core faculty. The long years of service of Colonel Richmond and Lieutenant Colonels Hodgin, Marshall, and Groseclose and Major Pace have been mentioned, but there were numerous other dedicated men who taught for many years. Those who were on the faculty for more than ten years were Edward Weber,

Plaque Honoring Colonel Richmond, Lieutenant Colonel Marshall, and Lieutenant Colonel Groseclose-Arrowood

Clyde Ghee, A. D. Stutzenberger, Miguel Zepeda, Nelson Hodgin, a 1926 KMI graduate, Lewis Gregg, Rawleigh Sallee, a 1927 KMI graduate, O. O. Pillans, Bartley Williams, Bernard Hewes, George Bales, Cromwell Hammock, a 1929 KMI graduate, Charles "Alex" Hodgin, a 1949 KMI graduate, and William Simpson.

In their years of service, they had learned the fine art of dealing with boys growing into young men. It is not surprising that the task of serving as tactical officers fell to those faculty members who had been at the school for years. Their years of experience made them the logical ones to review the reported misconduct of the cadets. Tactical officers in the 1950s were usually Williams, Bales, Hewes, Marshall, and Pace. These men probably had heard every excuse possible for a cadet being mistakenly stuck.

Ben Hewes Hears a Cadet's Story—Young

A number of other long-term members of the staff were Mrs. Hammock, the school librarian for more than ten years. Miss Mary Reichspfarr, known to every cadet simply as Miss Mary, was the cashier and social secretary. The school nurse, Evelyn "Maw" Fowler, ran the school's small infirmary and tended to minor illnesses and injuries.

Two men who were extremely important to the cadets and their daily lives were Norman "Kappy" Kapfhammer and Mr. E. T. Scoggins. Kappy ran the school's quartermaster store, where uniform items and other essentials could be purchased. But more importantly, he was responsible for the delivery of the mail to the cadets. Mr. Scoggins ran the dugout, located in the basement of A Barracks, where various food items could be purchased at specified times during the day.[287]

Another factor that added stability to KMI was the support of the school by the alumni who sent their sons to the school.

Miss Mary Reichspfarr-Reichspfarr

---

[287] Information compiled from numerous *Sabers* and *Catalogs*.

During the 1954 school year for example, 14 percent of the cadet corps was related to former KMI cadets. Twenty-one cadets were the sons of alumni, seventeen were brothers of former cadets, seven were nephews, and one was the great-grandson of a graduate. The fact that alumni sent their sons to KMI clearly indicates that they firmly believed that there were definite benefits to be gained by the education and training their sons would receive.[288] In addition, friends of alumni sent their sons to KMI based upon the perceived advantages an education at the school offered.

Kappy Helps Unload the KMI Special—Morgan

In 1967, the administration instituted a new system called the board of control which was intended to oversee the Rat system. When a new cadet refused to perform the duties required of him or if the old man was overly persistent, a full report was to be written out and turned into a designated member of the faculty. There were rumors that there would be a Rat system during the Florida term. There is no indication in any of the records as to what had prompted the change in policy or what impact the change had on the operation of the Rat system.

At the same time the administration was trying to deal with the Rat system, it was still struggling to control the smoking by cadets. In order for underclassmen to smoke legally, they had to carry a smoking card or permit. Seniors were free to smoke if they so desired. Presumably, to obtain a smoking card, the cadet had to have the written permission of his parents. In previous years, all cadets who smoked had to have a permission letter from their parents. It would be interesting to know how many of the cadets who smoked actually had their parent's permission.[289]

---

288   The *Kentucadet*, Vol. XXX, No. 2, December 1954, p. 15.
289   The *Kentucadet*, Vol. XXIII, No. 1, October 1967.

A number of graduates saw service in the Vietnam War, but the exact numbers will never be known. As far as can be determined, four graduates were killed in action in Southeast Asia. A large number of former cadets served with distinction in various branches of the military during the conflict. Despite Major Seibert's rather pessimistic view of the value of the ROTC program, a few graduates would pursue military careers. However, KMI was always a college preparatory school in the twentieth century. In February 1971, Major Hodgin reported that 98 to 100 percent of the graduates entered a college of their choice after graduation.[290]

Apparently, the changing economy was having a significant impact on the ability of families to send their sons to KMI. In 1971, Dr. Simpson reported that most of the cadets came from families that fell in the upper-income level. The cost of attending had risen rapidly over the last few years, and consequently, many well qualified boys were unable to enroll. As a consequence, the school was considering a program to award scholarships to qualified applicants who could not pay the tuition.

There were several valid financial reasons that the decision had been made to discontinue the practice of going to Florida during the winter. The cost of moving the entire staff, faculty, and student body was extremely costly. In addition, there was a pressing need to expand the size of the school in Venice. The school's location in downtown Venice, surrounded by established businesses and homes, made that expansion almost impossible. Even if property could be found for expansion, the cost of acquiring it would have been prohibitive. A final financial consideration was that the entire faculty consisted of men, and the move to Florida caused many problems for their working wives.[291]

President Richard Nixon sent a telegram to KMI on the occasion of its 125th anniversary in 1970. His message read: "The faculty, the alumni, and the cadet corps can take deep pride in the long and honorable history of your fine school. In the century and a quarter since Kentucky Military Institute conducted its first classes, it has imparted to thousands of young men the advantages of an excellent education and the enduring qualities of leadership, integrity and devotion to the welfare of our country. The

---

[290] "The KMI Story," *The L&N Magazine*, February 1971.
[291] Ibid.

graduates, in their turn, have contributed richly to the strength and progress of America."[292]

On March 25, 1971, a letter addressed to parents, alumni, and friends of KMI was mailed by William Simpson. The letter announced what was simply unthinkable to most of those to whom it was addressed. Kentucky Military Institute would cease to exist after 126 years with the beginning of the 1971-1972 school year. After considering a number of options, the Board of Directors of KMI had voted unanimously to cease operations as a military school. The decision was prompted by a number of considerations. The primary issue was the changing attitude of the nation concerning the military. In addition, the change in the American family which now permitted the children to make decisions previously made by their parents had a significant impact on enrollment at the school. It was apparent to the board that only a limited number of young men were interested in attending a school that's basic premise was that military discipline was an important part of the educational process.

Although KMI's purpose was always primarily academic, the philosophy had always been that military discipline was the best possible supplement to a student's preparation for college and life. "Unfortunately, each year fewer people seem to accept this premise." The fact that military schools were facing a continual decline in enrollment was forcing a change in a number of military schools around the country.

From the time KMI was purchased by Colonels Richmond, Hodgin, and Marshall, the operation of the school had been under the control of a board. After Colonel Marshall sold his interest, the board consisted of Colonel Richmond, Mrs. Richmond, and Colonel Hodgin. Upon Colonel Richmond's death, Dr. Simpson took his place on the board. Diane Simpson would replace her mother upon her death. [293] The board of directors had waited for a change in the public attitude toward military preparatory schools. They had incurred debts in the hope of preserving the traditions of KMI, but it was no longer possible to continue to incur additional losses. The board had considered merging with other independent schools in the Louisville area, but a merger did not seem advisable. The board found itself left with only two choices: change

---

[292]   Ibid.

[293]   E-mail from William T. Simpson to the author, May 7, 2013.

the structure of the school or cease operations. The latter choice was unacceptable to the board.

After commencement in 1971, the name of the school would be changed to Kentucky Academy. The administrators felt that the time gained from the elimination of the military program would enable them to present an outstanding college preparatory program. "Since the current administrators of the school are educators, rather than military men, we can be quite comfortable in the new environment." Kentucky Academy would be a coeducational school. Only boys would be a part of the boarding school program. It was projected that the business structure of the academy would be nonprofit. The letter stated that schools could no longer survive solely on the revenues from tuition. Therefore, tax-deductible contributions would be necessary to continue the school's operations. It is interesting to note that the change from a proprietary school to a nonprofit institute was what Simpson had discussed in his 1966 address to the Association of Military Colleges and Schools.

The directors stated that operational help would be needed as well as capital improvement. The school needed a new gymnasium, a larger academic building, and a new dormitory, all of which could be named after an alumnus who contributed to make the new buildings possible.[294] Kentucky Academy would pay rent on the facilities on the Lyndon campus, and KMI was merged into the new school. This plan was adopted so that if any well-financed investors could be found to reopen KMI, it would still have been in existence since 1845. According to Dr. Simpson, Kentucky Academy was never able to pay any rent on the facilities. [295]

Harking back to the question that Simpson had posed in 1966, the KMI administrators had had the patience to wait for the change in attitude but not the financial resources. James Stephens raised the issue of KMI's demise when he wrote, "When the whole history of KMI is examined closely and objectively, a critical observer may note that the seeds of KMI's demise were planted in the soil at Farmdale by none other than the founder."[296] The fact that KMI was heralded as the "oldest privately owned" military school in the United States was always put forward with

---

[294] William T. Simpson, Letter to "Parents, Alumni and Friends of KMI," March 25, 1971.

[295] E-mail William T. Simpson to the author, May 7, 2013.

[296] Stephens, op. cit., p. 287.

a great deal pride; however, it would eventually be one of the primary factors in the closing of the school. Just as Simpson had predicted in 1966, it became financially impossible to maintain the school as a privately owned entity. Efforts to convert the school to a different type of financial organization came too late to save the institution, and it was forced to close its doors.

In an article entitled "Education: No More Parades," *Time* magazine described the demise of military boarding schools in the late 1960s. "Rising cost and high tuitions have hurt all private schools, particularly boys and girls boarding schools. The major military boarding schools, however, have lost enrollment for four years running. Last year's drop at 17 manor institutions was nearly 11%—more than three times the decline at other boarding schools for boys. Four military academies have shut down within the past three years; eleven have dropped their association with the military."[297] The article specifically mentioned KMI as one of the school dropping the military regimen.

On May 30, 1971, Cadet William Leslie Wolff became the last graduate of Kentucky Military Institute.[298]

---

[297] *Time*, "Education: No More Parades," September 6, 1971.
[298] www.kmialumni.org/last_cadet.ht.

Chapter X

THE END

On May 18, 1973, Dr. Simpson and Charles "Alex" Hodgin sent a letter to the alumni, announcing the merger of Kentucky Academy and Kentucky Country Day (KCD) school at the end of the school year. The merged school would operate on the campus of KCD and the boarding program at Kentucky Academy would close:

> This change marks the end of an era, and, naturally is a very sad occasion for those of us who were close to the old K.M.I. Please be assured that the management exhausted every possibility of continuing the boarding program before reaching the final decision. Declining enrollments and increased costs made it impossible to continue. We have maintained the operation with substantial deficits for several years in hope the national climate for boarding schools would change, but the change did not materialize.

Studies had been conducted to examine the potential of raising funds to continue the operation of Kentucky Academy. All of the studies projected that the funds that might be raised would fall far short of projected requirements. "Thus, there was no alternative but to terminate the program as it had been structured for so many years."[299]

---

[299] William T. Simpson and Charles A. Hodgin to Alumnus, May 18, 2973.

For several years during the 1970s, the Lyndon campus was the home of the Walden School. The Walden School was founded in 1975 by Dr. Edward F. Vermillion and utilized Ormsby Hall, the gymnasium, and the classrooms. In 1980, Walden School moved into the Stivers Elementary school building, and the campus once again stood vacant.[300]

The Last Fire   Green

On Memorial Day weekend of 1982, the last major fire to strike KMI destroyed the interior of Ormsby Hall. The fire was the result of vandalism by two juveniles who were eventually arrested. The interior of Ormsby and the roof were extensively damaged by the fire. The exterior walls remained intact, and the burned structure stood in ruins until it was purchased, restored, and began a new life as the administrative building for Ten Broeck Hospital-KMI.

The *Louisville Courier Journal* announced on February 10, 1993, that a subdivision would be built on the old KMI property. The Canfield-Knopf Development Company had purchased 40.6 acres of land at the front of the property. Ten Broeck Hospital-KMI, which had opened on the back half of the property, would remain.

The School Is for Sale—Arrowood

The plan was to build a 129-lot subdivision named Autumn Ridge. The construction of the first 43 homes was to begin in July and take a year to complete. The houses were expected to sell for about $170,000. Most of the homes would be two stories and built of brick. The developer

---

[300] http://en.wikipedia.org/wiki/Walden_Schol_(Kentucky) and e-mail from William T. Simpson to the author, January 1, 2013.

expected that there would be three to four homes per acre. Entrance to the development would be through the old KMI front gate and down the tree-lined drive.[301]

After KMI ceased its winter trips to Venice in 1970, the buildings stood vacant for a few years. Eventually, the buildings would be sold to various groups who would make extensive renovations in order to convert them for commercial use. The Venice Hotel was purchased in 1981 by Far South Developers Inc. The developers renovated and

The Venice Hotel Patio—Morgan

restored it to its original state and converted it into a retirement residence known as Casa de Venice. In 1988, the Adult Care Management Corporation purchased the facility and renamed it Park Place. The San Marco underwent extensive remodeling that converted the rooms on the second and third floors into condominiums. The transition was accomplished by converting two or three of the rooms into modern living units. On the first floor, more than twenty shops and businesses would utilize the space. The walls of the first floor contain a large amount of information and memorabilia from the KMI years.

The gymnasium was acquired by the Venice Little Theatre in 1972. Over the years, extensive renovations have increased the original seating from 286 to 432 seats in the Mainstage and 90 in Stage II. The facility also contains a number of classrooms and rehearsal spaces. In 2008, the name was changed to the Venice Theatre

The Venice Theatre—Young

---

[301] "Subdivision Plan for Old KMI Site In Lyndon Spurs Memories, Regrets," Louisville *Courier Journal*, February 10, 1993.

because they were no longer "Little."[302] The large drill and athletic field between Tampa Avenue and Venice Avenue was converted into a large municipal parking lot and Centennial Park.

The Nerve Center Is Quiet—Arrowood

A Barracks—Arrowood

A Room in "A"
Barracks—Morgan

Second Stoop "A"
Barracks—Morgan

The Flag Still Flies in
Lyndon—Young

302 http://www.venicestage.com/indea.php/about-venice-theatre/history.html.

CONCLUSION

———◆———

On May 27, 1973, Dr. Harry Lee Bailey, the last president of the KMI Alumni Association, addressed the Kentucky Academy graduating class. After thanking the many faculty and staff members who had made KMI an outstanding school, Harry concluded,

> I do not know what the future holds for this beautiful campus. I feel sure that as I drive out the lane today, I leave this place for the last time, as I shall always remember it. It is my hope, and the hope of many members of the Cadet Corps, that at least a portion of the parade ground would be preserved as a playground or park, as a memorial to the Cadets who once marched there.
>
> Hopefully, K.M.I. may be a reality once again someday, somewhere else. But if that is not to be, and if a portion of the parade ground is preserved—should you go there early in the spring on a crisp bright Sunday afternoon—stop and listen for a moment. If you listen closely, surely you will hear the Adjutant shout, "Sound Adjutants Call!"—and the bugles will sound—for there the spirit of the Corps of the Kentucky Military Institute will march forever. And may the memory of that Corps never fade.

Harry was right. The corps of cadets is on the plain. The colors are uncased, and the guidons snap softly in the breeze. The corps waits patiently for the last cadet to join the formation. When he finally arrives and finds his place in the ranks, the command "Pass in review!" will carry down the line. With that command, the corps of cadets of Kentucky Military Institute will march into history.

Appendix I

---·←·---

BEST COMPANY

1906	A Company, Paul Long, Captain
1907	B Company, A. G. Foster, Captain
1908	A Company, George Sengel, Captain
1909	A Company, Frank Peak, Captain
1910	
1911	A Company, Marshall Giles, Captain
1912	A Company, Andrew Edministon, Captain
1913	A Company, James K. Ward, Captain
1914	B Company, Jack Duke, Captain
1915	B Company, William A. Park, Captain
1916	
1917	B Company, John Graham, Captain
1918	B Company, Harry Dixon, First Lieutenant
1919	B Company, R. F. McEldowney, Captain
1920	A Company, C. H. Cuthbertson, Captain
1921	C Company, Hugh Craddock, Captain
1922	C Company, Albert Ebersole, Captain
1923	C Company, Ted Broecker, Captain
1924	A Company, Earl Runyon, Captain
1925	School Closed
1926	B Company, Albert Early, Captain
1927	C Company, Dwight Leffingwell, Captain
1928	A Company, William Shouse, Captain
1929	C Company, Lloyd Ray, Captain
1930	B Company, Willis Lea, Captain
1931	C Company, Leon Hirsch, Captain

1932	B Company, Rufus Lazzell, Captain
1933	B Company, Samuel Lynch, Captain
1934	C Company, Price Powell, Captain
1935	C Company, Stanley Shapoff, Captain
1936	Band Company, Bodley Booker, Captain
1937	C Company, Carroll Eddie, Captain
1938	B Company, Clifford Cornell, Captain
1939	C Company, Paul Swetland, Captain
1940	C Company, William Hoblitzell, Captain
1941	B Company, Lawrence Haeger, Captain
1942	B Company, Robert Lazzell, Captain
1943	D Company, James Vest, Captain
1944	B Company, George Abt, Captain
1945	D Company, Robert Puryear, Captain
1946	B Company, Ted Jenks, Captain
1947	B Company, Richard Vinton, Captain
1948	D Company, William Francis, Captain
1949	D Company, William Well, Captain
1950	A Company, Roy Ferry, Captain
1951	B Company, John Poulter, Captain
1952	Band Company, Phil Farmer, Captain
1953	E Company, Donald Karem, Captain
1954	A Company, Joseph Gandolfo, Captain
1955	Band Company, George Rice, Captain
1956	C Company, Thomas Hanshaw, Captain
1957	A Company, Ronald Beckett, Captain
1958	D Company, Hugh Robbins, Captain
1959	D Company, Joe Wells, Captain
1960	D Company, Gary Juengling, Captain
1961	
1962	B Company, David Clarence Meyer, Captain
1963	B Company, John F. Michael Cunningham, Captain
1964	C Company, Robert Putnam Hulbert, Captain
1965	D Company, Terry Daspit, Captain
1966	A Company, Mark Glassmeyer, Captain
1967	D Company, James Aldous, Captain
1968	A Company, James McHendry, Captain
1969	C Company, John M. Jones, Captain
1970	B Company, Steve Hater, Captain
1971	B Company, William Brent Rice, Captain

Appendix II

—◆—

Enrollment

Year	Total Students	Post graduate	Junior School	Graduates	Year	Total Students	Post graduate	Junior School	Graduates
1847					1879	75			
1848					1880	83			
1849					1881	80			
1850					1882	96			
1851	150			4	1883	106			
1852				7	1884	124			
1853				14	1885	106			
1854	139			12	1886	84			
1855				16	1887	44			
1856				12	1888				
1857				18	1889				
1858	154			28	1890				
1859				13	1891				
1860				8	1892				
1861	154			18	1893	37			4
1862					1894				4
1863					1895				6
1864					1896	40			3
1865					1897				2
1866					1898				2
1867					1899				3
1868	177			8	1900	74			3
1869	125			6	1901				6
1870	125			20	1902				2
1871	112			9	1903				4
1872	109			8	1904				2
1873					1905				4
1874					1906				5
1875	50			3	1907				6
1876	51			8	1908	99			10
1877	55				1909				6
1878	56				1910				14

Year	Total Students	Post graduate	Junior School	Graduates	Year	Total Students	Post graduate	Junior School	Graduates
1911				6	1942	267		6	77
1912				8	1943	300	24	12	91
1913				12	1944	297	4	21	67
1914				6	1945	288		19	75
1915	130			10	1946	296		20	62
1916				12	1947	301	4	18	71
1917				7	1948	294	9	11	80
1918				7	1949	316	10	25	89
1919	186			9	1950	284	7	29	77
1920				35	1951				
1921	160			39	1952	328	7	34	65
1922				19	1953	330	10	28	77
1923				23	1954	323	7	29	74
1924				16	1955	332		39	79
1925					1956	324	4	33	70
1926	153			28	1957	328		41	61
1927	175			41	1958	324		30	72
1928	131			41	1959	310		22	72
1929	175			39	1960	331		16	73
1930	158			52	1961	315		16	78
1931				37	1962	330		22	78
1932	167	5		54	1963	299			64
1933		11		48	1964	312			72
1934		1		50	1965	304			99
1935	166		20	53	1966	277			74
1936	199	12	23	53	1967	297			54
1937					1968	266			60
1938	221		24	60	1969	273			69
1939	213	8	13	64	1970	206			50
1940	248	18	19	64	1971	165			43
1941	242	13	10	69					

The numbers in this table are taken from a variety of different sources: students listed in a number of *Sabers*, a handwritten listing of the number of graduates salvaged from A Barracks, Simpson's History of KMI, and various catalogs.

The number of graduates increased dramatically when KMI became strictly a preparatory school. The number of graduates for the period from 1847 to 1924 shown in the table is 386. Certainly, that number was higher, but the numbers simply are not available. Once Colonel Richmond assumed control of the school and it became solely a preparatory school, the number of graduates increased dramatically. The total in the above table is 2,826, with two years missing. If you assume that the number of graduates in those years was approximately the same as the years around them, the total number of graduates would exceed 3,000.

Unfortunately, there is no accurate number for how many cadets attended KMI. Jim Stephens lists the names of more than 11,000 cadets in his book, but he was certain, as I am, that the list was not complete. There was a large turnover in the number of students that attended KMI in any given period. A member of the 1959 graduating class, seventy-two cadets, who attended for four years had more than 135 classmates in that four-year period.

Junior school classes were eliminated gradually; the last sixth grade class began in September 1952; the last seventh grade class began in September 1958; and the final eighth grade class entered in September 1961.

Appendix III

RANKING CADETS

1897	Oliver Howell	1926	Marcellus Green
1898	Matthew Tyler	1927	Madison Gardner/Ronald Currie
1899	Edward Riley	1928	Carlos Fish
1900	Hamilton O. Herr	1929	Leo K. Broecker
1901	Stephen H. Shallcross	1930	Joseph Goodson
	Edward H. Smith	1931	Alton J. Eline
1902	Harry Blackburn	1932	Robert C. Heckman
1903	McLean Nash	1933	Richard Crawmer
	John Hornsby	1934	Herman Dotson
1904	William H. Young	1935	Roger Lovelace
	Eli O. Jackson	1936	John W. Bertelsman
1905	Robert O. Poage	1937	Tom Bigelow
	N. W. Green	1938	Scott Pearson
	Sylvan R. Lowe	1939	Robert Montgomery
1906	N. W. Green	1940	Robert T. Richmond
	Ralph R. Seger	1941	George Roberts
	Willard L. Bentley	1942	David C. Jones
1907	Paul Long	1943	Henry Pennington
1943	Henry Pennington	1944	Alfred Alfs
1908	Alex Foster	1945	Malcolm Watt
	George Sengel	1946	Bernard Youngs
	Saul M. Bonavita	1947	Harris Howard
1909	Harry Peck	1948	Robert Schmidt
	William G. Powell	1949	William Schulz
1910	Benjamin H. Connor	1950	James Gwaltney

1911	W. Marshall Giles	1951	James Jarrell
	Meredith H. Yates	1952	William Houston, III
	William G. Powell	1953	Joseph Scales
1912	Andrew Edmiston	1954	Scott Beard
1913	James Clay Ward	1955	Harry Bailey
1914	W. Scott Hallenberg	1956	Perrin McGee
1915	Jack Duke	1957	Peter B. Crawford
1916	Franklin Beard	1958	Richard C. Stephenson
1917	Oscar R. Johnston	1959	Charles L. Getman
	John T. Graham	1960	I. Franklin Stalcup
1918	Thomas Doremus	1961	Joseph Bollert
	John Cooke	1962	L. Berkley Davis
	Thomas Shinn	1963	John C. Marlowe
1919	Thomas M. Kildow	1964	Edward Clay Keeton Jr.
	Henry F. Mosher	1965	Fred D. Toncray
	Rochester F. McEldownery	1966	John Welton Macauley Jr.
	John S. Humphrey	1967	Glenn Charles Hanks
1920	Basil Godden	1968	Leon B. Hirsh
1921	Delos Hibner	1969	John Joseph Murphy
1922	Allan Murray Beard	1970	Beverly Gordon Yeiser
1923	Harry B. Wadlington	1971	James M. Wander
1924	Ted Broecker		
1925	School Closed		

Appendix IV

———◆———

HONORS

O ne innate drive in every person is to achieve in some activity. Along with this is the inner satisfaction that is gained when public recognition is made of this achievement.

Part of the general program here at KMI is the planning of activities so that cadets will have this opportunity to achieve in some field of endeavor. We also realize that cadets like to be recognized for outstanding performance . . . 70 percent of the cadet corps received one or more awards! This is as it should be, for there are many fields in which a boy may do fine work if he will but only apply himself. We can only say that we on the staff and faculty are proud of these cadets and this fine record of achievement.

SPECIAL AWARDS

The Legion of Honor Award is made to a select number of senior cadets who best exemplified the ideals of the school. Character, leadership, and loyalty are qualities that are considered by the faculty committee who make the selections each year.

The J. Minor Ewing Progress Award is made to the cadet considered to have made the greatest all-around progress during his four years at KMI. The award was established by J. Minor Ewing, Class of 1921.

Valedictorian is the recognition of the cadet in the senior class having the highest scholastic average.

Student Council members are selected each year by vote of the cadet corps. This group has the duty of upholding and enforcing the honor code of the school.

ACADEMIC HONORS

Biscoe Hindman Medal is awarded to the cadet having the highest average in each of the high school classes. The award is made possible by an endowment fund created by Colonel Biscoe Hindman, Class of 1883.

William Kendrick Medal is presented to the student in the eighth grade who has the highest scholastic average. Presented by William Kendrick Sons of Louisville.

Seventh Grade Academic Medal is presented to the cadet having the highest scholastic average in the seventh grade.

Robert Myers Memorial English Medal presented to the cadet showing the most achievement in English. Presented by Florida Chapter to the Alumni of KMI in memory of Mr. Robert L. Myers, former director of admissions at KMI.

Bausch and Lomb Science Award is given to the cadet who has the highest average in science and in the estimation of the faculty, showing the greatest promise in the field of science.

Norvin Green History Trophy is awarded to the cadet having the highest grades in American history. Presented by Norvin Green, Class of 1950.

N. F. Green Mathematics Cup is awarded to the cadet having the highest average in all of his mathematics courses. Presented by N. F. Green of Louisville, Kentucky.

Cockrill Declamation Award is presented to the winner of the Annual Declamation Contest. Made possible by Jean Paul Cockrill, Class of 1951.

Improvement in Public Speaking Medal (Freshman-Sophomore) is presented to the cadet in the freshman or sophomore class in public speaking showing the greatest improvement.

Improvement in Public Speaking Medal (Junior-Senior) is presented to the cadet in the junior or senior class in public speaking showing the greatest improvement.

Harvard Club Award is given by the Harvard Club of Kentucky to the member of the junior class having the highest average in English.

The Dana Huoni Plaque is presented to the cadet doing the most outstanding piece of work on the yearbook staff. Plague is presented by Dana Huoni, Class of 1955.

The Lee Huoni Plaque is presented to the cadet who was the most outstanding on the staff of the school newspaper staff. Presented by Lee Huoni, x' 1948.

Photography Medals are awarded to cadets for outstanding work in photography.

Stevens Band Trophy is given to the member of the band showing the greatest improvement. Given by William Stevens, a patron of the school.

Huoni Choir Trophy is presented to the cadet in the choir showing the most improvement. Presented by Dr. and Mrs. J. S. Huoni.

Royce Orchestra Trophy is awarded to the cadet showing the greatest achievement and all-around musical proficiency in the dance band. Presented by George A. Royce, Class of 1940.

Time Magazine Awards are given to the cadets in each class scoring highest on the annual *Time* Magazine Current Affairs Tests.

The Clinton Kelly Medal is given to the cadet having the highest average in general science. Presented by Dr. C. W. Kelly.

Quill and Scroll Medals are awarded to cadets who have shown outstanding achievement in the field of journalism.

Library Service Medals are presented to those cadets who have performed in an outstanding manner as library assistants.

Choir Medals are presented to those members for excellent work in the choir during the year.

Gold Stars are presented to cadets having an average of 85 or better with no grade below 80 each month for the entire school year.

Silver Stars are presented to cadets having an average of 85 with no grade below 80 each month for one semester of the school year.

MILITARY HONORS

The Alumni Association Military Trophy is awarded to the company which has accumulated the greatest number of points in drill, athletics, scholarship, and general school activities. Three special drills are also held during the year at which time special judging is done of the military precision of each company. The name of the company and its commander are engraved on the trophy which is kept on exhibition at the school. The commander is also given a silver bowl to be retained as a permanent possession. This company is designated as the color company for the ensuing year and its members wear a citation cord on the left shoulder of the dress uniform.

Best Drilled Platoon Insignia is given to the members of the best platoon in the corps. This is based on ratings earned in the company competitions during the year. Members of the platoon are authorized to wear a gold shoulder loop.

Best Drilled Squad Patches are awarded to cadets in the squad winning the annual squad drill competition.

PMS&T Cups are given by the professor of Military Science and Tactics to the outstanding commissioned officer and to the outstanding noncommissioned officer in the corps. The award is based on superior proficiency in performance of military duties, military bearing, and leadership.

Best Drilled Cadet Trophy is presented to the cadet who is the winner in the annual drill competition. Presented by Mr. William Pettit, Class of 1947.

Master Sergeant Clyde Ghee Medal is given to the winner of the junior school best drilled cadet competition. Given by Master Sergeant Clyde Ghee, who, for sixteen years, was an instructor in ROTC at KMI.

Ungerleider Trophy is presented to the cadet judged to be the neatest during the school year. Presented by Hugh Ungerleider, Class of 1943.

Reserve Officers' Association Medal is presented to the cadet having achieved the highest academic average in the senior basic course of the ROTC program. The medal is presented by the Louisville Chapter of the Reserve Officers' Association.

ROTC Academic Achievement Wreath is awarded to the top ten present of the ROTC students in each class based on grades earned in Military Science and Tactics.

The Henson Trophy is awarded to the high point man on the rifle team. Sponsored by Arthur Henson, Class of 1951.

Expert Rifleman Badges are awarded for qualification firing on the range with the .22 caliber rifle.

Sharpshooter Badges are awarded for qualification firing on the range with the .22 caliber rifle.

Marksman Badges are awarded for qualification firing on the range with the .22 caliber rifle.

Distinguished Military Bars are awarded to cadets who have had high scholastic achievement in Military Science and Tactics, outstanding ability in drill, leadership, and military bearing and for best exemplifying the ideals of the ROTC program.

Military Proficiency Bars are awarded to any cadet who displays an outstanding degree of proficiency or skill in any phase of military activity, including personal appearance and neatness.

Neatest Cadet Bars are presented to the cadet winning one of the Neatest Cadet Competitions held during the school year.

Neatest Room Bars are awarded to cadets who have consistently maintained the neatest room on each stoop during any quarter of the school year.

Merit Bars and Good Conduct Bars are awarded to cadets who have had an outstanding record of conduct during one of the quarters of the school year.

ATHLETIC HONORS

The Head Trophy is given to the cadet who, in the estimation of the coaches of the school, is the most outstanding athlete of the year. The trophy is given by Mr. J. A. Head, who had three sons graduate from KMI.

The Hodgin Tennis Trophy is presented to the most outstanding tennis player in the school. Presented by Lt. Col. C. E. Hodgin, KMI commandant.

The Pruitt Trophy is presented to the top golfer in the school. Trophy sponsored by Mr. Rodman Pruitt, X'1944.

The Getschow Memorial Trophy is presented to the high point man on the track team. Trophy is presented by Mr. Roy M. Getschow in memory of his son, George Getschow, Class of 1937.

The Ray Aquatic Cup is presented to the cadet judged to be the most outstanding member of the swimming team. The cup is presented by Carl Ray, Class of 1927.

"K" Club Trophy is presented to a nonletter man who has been outstanding in the athletic program of the school. The award is given by the members of the Varsity "K" Club who vote on who should receive the award.

The Ralph Cohen Plaque is presented to the company with the greatest number of points in intramural athletic competition during the year. Presented by Ralph Cohen, Class of 1939.

The H. T. Riggs Junior School Tennis Trophy is presented to the winner of the Junior School tennis tournament. The trophy is presented by Mr. H. T. Riggs.

"K" Letters are given to cadets who are members of a varsity sports team. In addition to the letters, each cadet who has received a varsity letter for the first time is presented a "K" key. This is a gift of the alumni association of the school.

Distinguished Athlete Bars are awarded to athletes of the school that achieved in some outstanding manner in one or more of the sports.

The foreword and list of awards is taken from the cadet honors booklet for 1956.

SOURCES

A NOTE ON SOURCES

There are good collections of *Sabers* from the 1930s to 1971 at Kentucky Country Day and the Venice Museum and Archives. The University of Kentucky Archives has an almost complete collection of *Sabers*.

Ben Kaufmann has approximately 250 original photographs from the late nineteenth and early twentieth centuries. All have been scanned, and some appear in this history. In addition, there are a number of clippings with the photographs. All of the materials were salvaged from the campus long after the school closed.

The author is in possession of a number of items salvaged from the Lyndon campus by Jack Morgan, Class of 1957, in 1981. The items included a scrapbook that contains a number of photographs, *Listening Posts, Kayemeye Anvils*, and other paper items. The items also include a 1908 *Saber* and a box of letters written by Colonel Fowler to the parents of cadets.

The author has a card file which contains information on the more than 11,000 cadets who attended KMI and faculty members. The card file was originally maintained by the alumni association but was expanded by James Stephens when he was researching his history. The file contains information covering the years of attendance, birth dates, and other pertinent information. Also included in the files is some of the correspondence of Stephens while he was researching his history.

The author is in possession of seventy-three reels of 16mm movies that were taken by Captain Hammock in the late '40s and early '50s. The films were donated to the KMI alumni by Betty Kay Hammock Utley.

Individual issues of publications such as the *Kentucadet* and the *Kayemeye Anvil* are not listed here. Unfortunately, there is no complete collection of either publication. Only scatter copies of many other publications, such as the *Listening Post*, are available.

BOOKS

Porter E. Sargent, *A Handbook of the Best Private Schools of the United States and Canada*, 1915).

Andrews, Rod, *Long Gray Lines: The Southern Military School Tradition, 1839-1915,*Chapel Hill, University of North Carolina Press, 2001.

Backus, Jim *Rocks on the Roof*, New York, G.P. Putnam, 1958.

Barefoot, Daniel W. *General Robert F. Hoke: Lee's Modest Warrior*, Winston-Salem, John F. Blair, Publisher, 2001.

Bernard, Henry *Military Schools and Courses of Instruction in the Science and Art of War, in France, Prussia, Austria, Russia, Sweden, Switzerland, Sardina, England, and the United States*, New York, Greenwood Press, 1969.

Cadet Honors, 1956.

Cadet Honors, 1957.

Catalogue of Officers and Cadets of the Kentucky Military Institute, From September 12, 1853, to June 14, 1854, Frankfort, Kentucky., A.G. Hodges & Co., 1854.

Catalogue for the Kentucky Military Institute for 1867, Frankfort, Kentucky, S.I.M. Major Co., 1867.

Catalogue for the Kentucky Military Institute for 1868, Frankfort, Kentucky, S.I.M. Major Co., 1868.

Catalogue of the Officers and Cadets of the Kentucky Military Institute, From September 4, 1871, to June 6, 1872, Indianapolis, Indiana, Indianapolis Sentinel Printing Co., 1872.

Catalogue for the Kentucky Military Institute for 1873, Frankfort, Kentucky, S.I.M. Major Co., 1873.

Catalog for the Kentucky Military Institute, 1914.

Catalog for the Kentucky Military Institute, 1930.

Catalog for the Kentucky Military Institute, 1932

Catalog for the Kentucky Military Institute, 1933.

Catalog for the Kentucky Military Institute, 1936.

Catalog for the Kentucky Military Institute, 1937.

Catalog for the Kentucky Military Institute, 1952.

Catalog for the Kentucky Military Institute, 1955.

Conrad, James Lee, *The Young Lions: Confederate Cadets at War*, Columbia, University of South Carolina Press, 2004.

Cullum, George Washington, *Biographical Register of the Officers and Graduates of the U.S. Military Academy at West Point, N. Y. from Its Establishment in 1802 to 1890 with the Early History of the United States Military Academy*, 3 Volumes, Third Edition, Boston, Houghton, Mifflin Co., 1891.

Ellis, William E., *A History of Education in Kentucky*, Lexington, University of Kentucky Press, 2011.

Fleming, Walter L. (ed.), *General W.T. Sherman As College President*, Cleveland, The Arthur H. Clark Co., 1912.

——————, —————— *Louisiana State University, 1860-1896*, Baton Rouge, Louisiana State University Press, 1936.

Flynn, George Q., The Draft, 1940-1973, Lawrence, Kansas, University Press of Kansas, 1993.

——————, —————— Louis B. Hershey, *Mr. Selective Service*, Chapel Hill, University of North Carolina Press, 2011.

Green, Jennifer R., *Military Education and the Emerging Middle Class in the Old South*, New York, Cambridge University Press, 2008.

Krick, Robert E. L., *Staff Officers in Gray: A Biographical Register of the Staff Officers in the Army of Northern Virginia*, Chapel Hill, University of North Carolina Press, 2003.

Machoian, Ronald G., *William Harding Carter and the American Army, A Soldier's Story*, Norman, University of Oklahoma Press, 2006.

Melbourne A Century of Memories: The Melbourne Centennial Book, Published by the Melbourne Area Chamber of Commerce Centennial Committee, 1980.

Seibert, Donald A., *The Regulars: An Account of the Military Career of Colonel Donald A. Seibert, USA Ret.*, Victoria, BC, Trafford Publishing, 2010.

Settle, James W., *The Beanery: A Village Named Ormsby*, Brandon, Oregon, 2003.

Shofner, Jerrell H., *History of Brevard County*, Vols. I and II, Brevard Historical Commission, 1996.

Stephens, James D., *Reflections: A Portrait-Biography of the Kentucky Military Institute (1845-1971)*, Georgetown, Kentucky, Kentucky Military Institute, Inc., 1991.

The *Kayemeye Anvil*, bound volume for 1947-1948.
The *Kayemeye Anvil*, bound volume for 1945-1946.

LETTERS

Undated letter from R. T. P. Allen, "To the Friends and Patrons of the Kentucky Military Institute."
Undated letter from C. B. Richmond, "Speaking of Bargins."
Undated letter from C. B. Richmond, "We go to Florida to study, to work, and build health."
Undated letter from C. B. Richmond, "Does your local public school situation present a personal problem to you?"
Undated letter from C. B. Richmond, "A Heart-to-Heart Talk with Parents about Their Boys."
Letter from C. B. Richmond to M.G. Mature, July 10, 1929.
Letter from S. B. Marshall to M.G. Mature, April 24, 1929.
Letter from M. G. Mature to Colonel Richmond, October 29, 1928.
Letter from John H. Allen to Colonel C. B. Richmond, March 29, 1941.
Letter from C. B. Richmond to Alumnus, January 31, 1955.
Letter from O. O. Pillans to Dr. T. R. Young, February 10, 1955.
Letter to New Patrons of the Kentucky Military Institute, 1955-56 Session, August 9, 1955.
Letter from William T. Simpson to the author, January 27, 2012.
Letter from William T. Simpson to the author, February 27, 2012.
Letter from William T. Simpson to the author, October 6, 2012.
Letter, 1959, concerning Christmas vacation and weekend leave.
E-mail from William T. Simpson to the author, November 9, 2012.
E-mail from William T. Simpson to the author, November 22, 2012.
E-mail from William T. Simpson to the author, November 23, 2012.
E-mail from William T. Simpson to the author, December 3, 2012.
E-mail from William T. Simpson to the author, December 19, 2012.
E-mail from William T. Simpson to the author, January 1, 2013.
E-mail from William T. Simpson to the author, February 23, 2013.
Letter from Colonel Edmund L. Gruber, "A Statement to Our Patrons," February 2, 1920.
Letter from William T. Simpson and Charles A. Hodgin, May 18, 1973.
Letter from William T. Simpson and Charles A. Hodgin, March 25, 1971.

E-mail from Park A. Shaw to the author, January 29, 2013.
E-mail from Park A. Shaw to the author, January 30, 2013.
E-mail from Park A. Shaw to the author, January 31, 2013.
E-mail from Park A. Shaw to Bernard Dahlem, January 31, 2013.
E-mail from Park A. Shaw to the author, March 26, 2013.
E-mail from Bernard Dahlelm to the author, January 31, 2013.

ARTICLES

Allardice, Bruce, "West Points of the Confederacy: Southern Military Schools and the Confederate
Army." *Civil War History* 43, no. 4, December 1997, 310-331.
Alstetter, Mable and Gladys Watson, "Western Military Institute, 1847-1861," *Filson Club Historical. Quarterly,* 10, April, 1936, pp. 100-115.
M. J. Robards, "The School that Rides South with the Sun," *The L&N Employee's Magazine*, February 1951.
No Author, "The KMI Story," *The L&N Magazine*, February, 1971.
Miller, David and Charles Pate, "An Identified Cadet Trapdoor Rifle of the Kentucky Military Institute"
Military Collector and Historian (Journal of the Company of Military Historians), 62:4, Winter 2010.
Green, Jennifer R., "Networks of Military Educators: Middle-Class Stability and Professionalization in the Late Antebellum South," *Journal of Southern History*, Vol LXXIII, No. 1, February, 2007, pp.
"New K.M.I. Rises from Ruins of Old," The *Louisville Times*, no date, 1922.
Prunier, Tom, "Virginia's Military School Tradition," *Virginia Living*, February, 2005, pp. 118-123.
"The K.M.I. Steam Engine," *Scientific American*, Vol. XXIX, No. 22, November 29, 1873.
The *Venice News*, Friday, June 3, 1927—this issue is dedicated to the progress of Venice.
"150 Cadets Expected at K.M.I. to Reopen in Fall with Prof. J. H. Richmond on Its Staff," newspaper article, no paper, no date.
"Edison Science Building Dedication," The *New York Times*, May 28, 1913.

"Society at Palm Beach: Special to the New York Times," The *New York Times*, March 15, 1907.

"Boy Cadet Divorced," The *New York Times*, April 5, 1904.

"Special K.M.I. Section," *Sarasota Herald*, April 2, 1936.

"Education: No More Parades," *Time*, September 6, 1971.

"Burning of the Kentucky Military Institute," The *New York Times*, April 4, 1860.

ELECTRONIC SOURCES

Information on Chester C. Travelstead at http://www.ed.sc.edu/museum/travelstead.

Travelstead, Chester C., "The Year at the Kentucky Military Institute," http://www.unm.edu/~ddarling/V6.html.

Travelstead, Chester C., "Buttons are for Buttoning," http://www.unm.edu/~ddarling/v6v1s1.html.

Travelstead, Chester C., "Mr. Day, a Band Director not to be Forgotten," http://www.unm.edu/~ddarling/v6v2s1.html.

Travelstead, Chester C., "The President's Errant Brother," http://www.unm.edu/~ddarling/v6v4s1.html.

Travelstead, Chester C., "Join the Marines and See the World," http://www.unm.edu/~ddarling/v6v5s1.html.

Travelstead, Chester C., "I thought you Said We were Invited to Supper," http://www.unm.edu/~ddarling/v6v7s1.html.

Travelstead, Chester C., "Didn't anyone give you the Signal," http://www.unm.edu/~ddarling/v6v6s1.html.

Travelstead, Chester C., "Victor John Mature and Gilmore James Backus," http://www.unm.edu/~ddarling/v6v8s1.html.

Travelstead, Chester C., "No School on Monday," http://www.unm.edu/~ddarling/v6v3s1.html.

NONPUBLISHED SOURCES

Baker, Dean Paul, "The Partridge Connection: Alden Partridge and Southern Military Education," Ph.D. dissertation, Chapel Hill, University of North Carolina, 1986.

Simpson, William Taylor, "A History of the Kentucky Military Institute During the Nineteenth Century, 1845-1900, July 1954.

Simpson, William Taylor, "The Next Fifty Years," Address to the Association of Military Colleges and Schools, March 29, 1966.

Abstract of Title for Eau Gallie property from earliest public records of Brevard Co. Fla., to and including the 24th day of May AD 1947.

Kentucky Historic Resources Inventory, Maghers Glass/Ormsby Hall, Jefferson County Office of Historic Preservation, September 29, 1979.

National Register of Historic Places Inventory, Stewart Home School, Nomination Form, June 3, 1976.

National Register of Historic Places Inventory, Col. R. T. P. Allen House, Nomination Form, July 10, 1979.

Scrapbook prepared by Thomas Kildow, KMI Class of 1919.

Scrapbook prepared by Murray Allen Beard, KMI Class of 1922.

Scrapbook prepared by Benjamin Franklin Beard, KMI Class of 1916.

Scrapbook prepared by Henry C. Talmadge, KMI Class of 1920.

Scrapbook prepared by Jack Morgan, KMI Class of 1957.

Student file and application of Victor John Mature, September 10, 1928.

Telephone conversation between the author and Betty Kay Hammock Utley, January 25, 2013.

Webb, Lester Austin, "The Origin of Military Schools Founded in the United States in the Nineteenth Century," Ph.D. dissertation, Chapel Hill, University of North Carolina, 1958.

PHOTOGRAPH CREDITS

The photographs that appear in this work are from a number of sources. At the end of each caption, the one word indicates the source. Young—the author; Kaufmann—Ben Kaufmann; Morgan—Jack Morgan; Arrowood—Larry Arrowood; Brinker—Gerry Brinker; McDonald—Jim McDonald; Venice—Venice Museum and Archives; Simpson—William T. Simpson; Beard—Murray Allen Beard and Franklin Beard; Tullis—Jim Tullis; Reichspfarr—Mary Reichspfarr; and Green—Norvin Green.